Snakebit!

By

Andrew Soyars

Dedicated to all those who have fallen victim to the snake…
but even more so to the Antidote!

"And these signs will accompany those who believe: In my name they will drive out demons; they will speak in new tongues; they will pick up snakes with their hands; and when they drink deadly poison, it will not hurt them at all; they will place their hands on sick people, and they will get well."

Mark 16:17,18

"I have given you authority to trample on snakes and scorpions and to overcome all the power of the enemy; nothing will harm you."

Luke 10:19

"Paul gathered a pile of brushwood and, as he put it on the fire, a viper, driven out by the heat, fastened itself on his hand. When the islanders saw the snake hanging from his hand, they said to each other, "This man must be a murderer; for though he escaped from the sea, Justice has not allowed him to live." But Paul shook the snake off into the fire and suffered no ill effects."

Acts 28:3-5

All Scripture references taken from the NIV Bible unless
otherwise noted.
Copyright © 1973, 1978, 1984 by International Bible Society.

Copyright © 2007 Andrew C. Soyars
All rights reserved.

ISBN: 978-0-6151-5624-8

Author's note

I've had the idea for this book for sometime, and finally got around to putting it down on paper. I have to admit, that as it progressed, it took a whole different direction from the one I had originally intended! I feel like I've learned a lot about the world we live in during the course of this book, but of course, I still don't have all the answers. In fact, I have very few. I think I have acquired a much better understanding of what it is to be "snakebit," though, and that's the first step toward getting free of the snakes. Hopefully, by the time you finish this book, you too, will be a little closer to finding your freedom in Christ.

This book isn't meant to be an exhaustive study on the subject, but rather, it contains some ideas (that may be new to you) designed to get you headed in the right direction in your own study. Your teacher should be the Holy Spirit through God's own Word. The reason for this is fairly simple. Some of the things contained within these pages may lead you to make decisions that call for a great deal of faith. Those decisions, as well as your faith, shouldn't be based on another man's writings, but on the Word of God speaking to you and your heart. I can have faith only for myself, and what I believe He's told me. The same is true for you.

These pages are meant to make you aware of what might be called "The Great Deception." It's not a man-made deception, though man definitely plays a role in it. It's the deception of the serpent. We've all been snakebit and most of us don't even realize it. That's why this book was written. To help make you aware. What you do (or don't do) with it is entirely your choice. My intent is not to persuade you to do anything or not, simply to make you aware of the "spell" of the serpent that we've found ourselves taken captive by. It is your choice to continue in bondage…it is your choice to find your freedom through faith in Jesus Christ.

My job is simply to sound the trumpet…

1.

The naked man lay in the cool grass beneath the shadows of the trees that lined the quiet brook. His head and shoulders propped comfortably against the chest of a sleeping lion, he watched the woman, also naked, wading in the shallow water. From time to time, she would giggle softly as a tiny fish wriggled between her toes, as though giving her little fishy hugs. Neither was aware of the pair of sinister eyes that watched from the heavy brush.

The man reached back and gently scratched the belly of the slumbering cat, and felt its chest rumble deep inside as it began to purr. Both man and lion were quite content. The man would have been surprised to know of the danger that lurked behind the eyes in the bushes. For as long as he had lived here…in fact, for as long as he had lived…he had never known danger. Nor had the woman. Neither had known anything but bliss, here in this paradise. But that would soon change. And only the mind behind the eyes in the bushes had any inkling of what was about to happen.

The man rose to his feet, ruffled the feline's mane and began walking toward the woman in the brook. Without waking, the lion stretched its legs and paws, and rolled over, arching its belly toward the late afternoon sky. The woman looked up as the man approached and smiled. Without hesitating, the man stepped into the water. Perfect, as always.

He held out his hand and she took it in hers. The small fish around her feet had been joined by others, and they rushed over to greet the man, darting in and out between the four human feet that stood in the middle of their playground. The eyes in the bushes watched it all. They watched as the man and his wife slowly waded in his direction. And they waited…gleaming with anticipation. A forked tongue snaked out between scaly lips, testing the air…tasting the human scent. And still, the man and the woman were unaware.

But soon. Yes, soon they would be painfully aware.

The eyes watched as the man and the woman walked slowly back toward the edge of the brook and stepped onto the grass. The lion lazily raised its head and rolled to its feet. Together, the three of them disappeared into the lengthening shadows of the bushes, the leaves slowly closing behind them. But the eyes weren't worried. They would be back tomorrow.

They came here every day.

2.

There had been a time, somewhere in eternity past, that things had been different. Before the "incident" that left him so disfigured and scarred. Back when he still served the Master. Sure, he was clever at disguising his features. In fact, when he had the time and the desire to do so, even now he could make himself look quite appealing. But there was no way to disguise the hatred. That was always there, no matter what mask he wore.

He had once been a creature of unsurpassed beauty and wisdom, so he had been told. Back then, of course. Before the "incident." At first, he had been flattered by the attention he used to receive, and by the compliments and the stares as he passed. The Master had even seen fit to give him his own paradise. Much like the one here. Actually, this one was a mere copy of the one he had come from. Or rather, the one he had been driven from…back in eternity past. Remembering simply fueled his rage. Paradise! The very thought of the word…

In any event, as time passed in that place of timelessness, he had fallen victim to himself. He had enjoyed so many riches and blessings, so much success and adoration that he had become convinced that he was indeed a superior being. And pride had slipped in. That, of course, had led to the "incident."

In his puffed up mind, he had realized that he was, at least in his own opinion, much more capable of being the Master than was the Master, Himself. And because of his arrogance and pride, he rebelled. It was a well-planned assault. He was, after all, a creature of great wisdom. He had also recruited a fairly good-sized army, which naturally, he would lead. And the others…as soon as the battle began and they saw him in all his splendor and majesty, leading the victorious troops against the Master's house, surely they would join in.

Ironically, it wasn't mistreatment that caused him to rebel. In fact, the Master had been far too kind and had shown him far too much favor. But the Master was still only the Master. He knew deep down inside that the others would prefer his own kingship to that of the Master. Who wouldn't? After all, just look at him! Imagine all that he could accomplish if the throne was his! And so…

As it turned out, things didn't go according to plan. Nothing, in fact, went according to plan. While he would never admit defeat, he had greatly underestimated the power of the Master. He was surprised to find, in his own twisted mind, that it was almost equal to his own. (He had so convinced himself of his superiority, that even in defeat he claimed victory, empty though it was!).

His defeated armies were cast into the dungeons and bound with chains. Tormented, even, for their role in the rebellion. He, himself, had been cast out of the Master's presence and into the wilderness. Banished, like a child! The shame was horrendous. From honor and glory, to…this. Disgrace. Defeat. Unbearable humiliation. But that was about to change. He could sense it…he could taste it! It was about to change, and it was all because of the man and the woman.

Victory was near…and he could hardly wait!

3.

It was late afternoon. The man and the woman would be along soon. Today, he would put his plan into action. Today, he would not hide in the bushes watching. He had watched enough. He had been observing the man and the woman for quite some time now. Long enough to know everything about them there was to know. Their habits and mannerisms. The way they walked and talked. What they spoke about. When they ate their meals. What they ate. He knew their voices and to some degree could even guess at their very thoughts. He even knew the purr of the lion that often accompanied the man. Yes, he had watched them for a long, long time.

Today, he would simply be resting in the shade of the trees when they arrived. In the spot the man liked to rest in after working in the garden all day. They came here, the man and woman, every day. To the brook. She would wade around and splash with the fish while he would prop himself against his lazy, useless lion and watch. Sometimes the man would join her in the brook and they would play their stupid little games in the water, or chase each other along the bank. He felt a jolt of revulsion as the voices of the man and woman laughed and giggled in his mind. He could hardly contain his disgust and hatred.

He shuddered violently, as though trying to shake the images of the man and woman from his mind. He would much rather envision what was coming. *Those* images, he could enjoy. He smiled to himself and rolled over in the soft grass. For just a moment, the slits in his eyes blinked rapidly as he found himself staring into the afternoon sun. Then he lay there, simply staring at the sun with his tiny slits, as if in defiance of the sun itself.

Nearby, he heard the rustling of the bushes. The man and the woman. He smiled to himself and stretched. This shouldn't be too difficult. Their voices were low, no doubt babbling nonsense to each other in meaningless conversation. That's pretty much how he summed up the humans. Meaningless. Useless. Except for one thing. Getting back at the Master. For that, they would be extremely useful. He quickly put on his "pretty face" as the rustling of the bushes grew closer.

"Hello," said the woman as she broke into the clearing. She hadn't seemed surprised in the least to see him reclining under the tree. There was no reason to be surprised here. All creatures were under the dominion of her husband. In fact, the very land was under his rule. No danger. No fear. Just perfect bliss. How putrid! But that would soon change. And then, *then* there would be a new master of this world. The one who *truly* deserved it. *Then*, the puny disgusting little particle called man would serve *him*. The fools! He smiled his most dazzling smile.

"Hello," he replied. "Beautiful day, isn't it?"

"Have you ever seen one that wasn't?" the woman giggled.

"Hello there!" The man broke through the bushes, followed by the lion.

"Good afternoon. That's a handsome cat by your side."

The man smiled and nodded as the woman headed for the brook.

"You're rather handsome yourself," the man replied. "I've never seen a creature yet that wasn't. Our God is amazing isn't He? I believe I stay in a constant state of wonder! Every day I find something new to be astounded by!"

The man laughed as he ruffled the lion's mane. The lion

leaned over and began nibbling on the leaves of a nearby bush as the man stroked his furry ears.

The mention of the Master's name caused the beady eyes to contract, ever so slightly, and he could feel the flicker of fury that flashed through them, but neither the man nor the lion seemed to notice or care. He swallowed the bile that rose almost uncontrollably in his throat, and concentrated on speaking in an even voice.

"Yes, that God, He's something alright."

He forced a smile and willed all of his beauty and splendor into it. He could tell the man was impressed. He watched as the man joined his wife in the brook, the couple gently splashing one another's naked body in the cool water. Laughing. Giggling. Enjoying the afternoon and each other. This wouldn't be so hard. Not at all.

They spent the afternoon together, the four of them. Himself, the man and woman, and that lazy cat that always followed the man. Seemed all the loathsome creature did was eat, sleep and purr. He found himself wondering if there was enough vegetation in the garden to feed this beast. He had been invited to join them for the evening, but he had declined. He knew how they spent their evenings. Walking in the cool of the day with...

His mind couldn't stop the string of curses and loathing that went through it. And if he could have stopped them, he would have chosen not to. How he hated that Name! How he despised that Person! *God!* He spat, as though the act of spitting would get rid of the taste of that name. He shuddered. No. No, thank you, he had replied. Not today. Tomorrow, perhaps.

Yes, he would be there tomorrow.

4.

As the sun rose the next morning, the creature was almost beside himself with an excited expectation. Today would be the day. Gaining the trust of the man and woman would be too easy. They had never had any reason to distrust anyone or anything before. He was quite sure they wouldn't even know how to distrust…the imbeciles. There was a part of him that even wished, just a little, that this whole venture might be a bit more challenging.

He made his way quickly through the brush. He knew just where to find the humans at this part of the day. They would be in the middle of the garden. He chuckled to himself, his mind racing with anticipation. He paused and listened. Just ahead he could hear the river that watered the garden. That's exactly where he expected to find them. The foolish woman would be swimming in the river. The lazy cat would be nibbling leaves from the bushes along the bank, and the arrogant man would be picking fruit from the trees for their morning meal.

Just before he reached the clearing, he again put on his "pretty face." He practiced his most charming smile a time or two, parted the brush and stepped into the clearing. The lion paid him no attention. There it was, with its face buried in the brush, nibbling away. Just as he had known it would be. The woman, of course, was in the water. And the man. There he was picking fruit for himself and his wife. Just as he had known.

"Good morning!" the man said as he looked up.

"Hello," the creature replied with his practiced smile. "Another beautiful day!"

"Yes, it is! Would you care for a little fruit this morning?" the man asked. "As you know, there's plenty."

The man offered the creature an apple as he called for his wife. From the middle of the river she looked in his direction and immediately began swimming for shore with a ridiculously big smile on her face. The creature smiled and nodded at the woman and watched her wave back. Such simple creatures they were!

The creature politely refused the apple and engaged the man in conversation as his wife approached. Watching her from the corner of his eye slits, he spoke again as she drew near.

"You know, I have no taste for apples this morning, but…" the creature paused for just a moment. "What sort of fruit might that be? It looks absolutely delicious!"

He smiled his practiced smile once again, as he nodded toward a towering tree that stood near the mouth of the river.

The man smiled his stupid smile.

"Don't these humans ever get tired of being so repulsive?" the creature thought to himself.

. "I'm not sure what sort of fruit it is. I've never eaten any of it. Nor has my wife," the man replied.

The woman, her naked body still dripping water, spoke.

"The Lord told us we can't eat from that tree."

"Now the serpent was more crafty than any of the wild animals the Lord God had made. He said to the woman, "Did God really say, 'You must not eat from any tree in the garden'?"

The woman said to the serpent, "We may eat fruit from the trees in the garden, but God did say, 'You must not eat fruit from the tree that is in the middle of the garden, and you must not touch it, or you will die.'" (Gen. 3:1-3).

The creature smiled his finest smile of all.

"You will not surely die," the serpent said to the woman. "For God knows that when you eat of it your eyes will be opened, and you will be like God, knowing good and evil." (Gen. 3:4).

The creature spoke in a soothing, reassuring voice and walked over to the huge tree at the mouth of the river, it's branches slightly bowed from the weight of the abundant fruit. The man and the woman were just behind him, and the grazing lion glanced casually in their direction.

As the creature approached the tree, a slight hiss escaped from his throat, danced over his forked tongue and slipped into the suddenly still air of the garden, though neither the man, nor the woman was quite close enough to hear. Almost. But not quite. He smiled again, reached up and plucked a plump piece of fruit from the tree.

"See?" he asked as he held up the fruit. He raised it over his head and grinned. "As you can see, no harm has been done, and I am perfectly well."

The lady inched closer, with her husband on her heels. Her eyes studied the creature, then the fruit…and then the creature again. Could it be he was telling the truth? Her mind was suddenly flooded with thoughts. Maybe God really was trying to keep something from them. Maybe the fruit really wouldn't bring death. The creature was surely enough alive, though he held a piece of it in his hand.

"When the woman saw that the fruit of the tree was good for food and pleasing to the eye, and also desirable for gaining wisdom, she took some and ate it. She also gave some to her husband, who was with her, and he ate it." (Gen. 3:6).

Several things happened all at once at that precise moment in time. As the woman slowly raised the fruit to her lips, the creature inched a bit closer. As she sank her teeth into the flesh of the fruit, his façade of beauty melted away to reveal the hideous form that lay beneath. In the blink of an eye, his scaly body had coiled around her naked legs, and as she bit into the fruit, his fangs pierced her tender thigh and he injected his lethal poison.

She handed the fruit to the man, unaware just yet, of the fatal wound she had suffered. The man never saw the monstrous creature wrapped around his wife's legs. He never saw the fangs fastened to her thigh. His eyes were fixed, instead, on her eyes. Watching. Waiting. He watched his wife slowly chew, swallow, then look up at him as though waiting. As he watched, as he waited with her, he reached out to take the fruit. He raised it to his own lips. He closed his eyes…and he ate.

Neither saw the creature spring toward the man. Neither was aware that as the man raised the fruit to his lips, the creature was now coiled around the man's legs. Neither was aware, that as the man ate, he too, suffered a deadly bite to the thigh. The venom was just entering his bloodstream.

The man opened his eyes and looked at the creature, who was again standing in all his beauty before them…smiling that smile…watching. Neither the man, nor the woman noticed the tiny droplets of blood that now clung to the creature's brilliant white teeth. For the first time ever, when the man and the woman looked at each other, they realized the other was naked. For the first time ever, they each felt shame at their own nakedness.

Had the man's eyes been open when he bit into the fruit, and had he been, for whatever reason, watching the lion at the very instant that his teeth broke the skin of that fruit, he would have been close enough to see an interesting phenomenon. For at that very moment, the lion paused from his grazing and looked toward the man…and as the man took the bite, a light flashed in the lion's eyes, ever so briefly, then just as quickly, it flickered out…and a new look took it's place.

The lion's lips slowly curled back, and for the first time ever, a low quiet growl began in its belly and began to work it's way through the solid, muscular chest. The low rumbling sound continued for, what seemed like several moments, until the great beast finally threw its head back, parted its lips and the gurgling snarl became a mighty roar that shattered the silence and shook the very ground of the garden. It tossed its head violently, as though trying to shake off something that was clinging to its mane, glared menacingly at the man and the woman, and leapt into the dense underbrush.

And for the first time ever, the man felt fear. Along with shame, it would be an emotion that he would come to know well. Though neither the man, nor the woman could see it, it was at that very moment in time that even the plants of the garden began to decay, as the poison spread from the humans to everything else on earth.

"The creation waits in eager expectation for the sons of God to be revealed. For the creation was subjected to frustration, not by its own choice, but by the will of the one who subjected it..." (Rom. 8:19-21).

Even as the man swallowed, the fruit slipped from his fingers. There was a flood of strange new feelings that coursed through his body as his bloodstream carried the venom even to his very heart. With the shame and the fear came, for the first time ever, anger, guilt and even jealousy, as he watched the creature eyeing his naked wife in a way that he had never before seen. The man found that he didn't much care for these new feelings, but...it was too late. As time passed, he would find there were many others that were just as undesirable.

"Then the eyes of both of them were opened, and they realized they were naked; so they sewed fig leaves together and made coverings for themselves." (Gen. 3:7).

Neither the man, nor the woman realized it at the moment. It was far beyond their comprehension. Neither could know the significance of what had just happened. But those who came after would figure it out at some point in time. Those who came after would have the benefit of history to study. Those who came after would come to realize that, at that very moment in time, the world's first man...and the world's first woman...had just suffered from the world's very first snakebite.

For the very first time in the history of the world, the very first humans had been *snakebit!* The venom would travel to, and through, their offspring. And the venom would travel through time. It would affect every human being that would ever live from that point on.

Except one.

The Antidote.

5.

Ever since that first snakebite, we humans have been getting nibbled on day in and day out. Most of us don't realize it, but it's true. We are the serpent's "chew toy." Some of us have been bitten so often, and have so many fang-holes in our flesh, we look like sponges! Just like Adam and Eve, we are seldom aware of the danger until it's too late. And, like Adam and Eve, often we're not even aware that we've been snakebit!

The question may arise, that if we're not aware that we've been bitten, why is there a problem? If the snakebites don't affect us any more than that, everything should be ok…right? The thing is, whether you realize you've been bitten or not, the venom is still running through your system. You're still dying from those snakebites, whether you feel them or not. And once you're dead, you'll still be just as dead…whether you felt them or whether you didn't. Physically, and, more importantly, spiritually.

Keep in mind it's not the snakebite that does the harm. The death is in the venom. The bite itself may pierce the skin a little, but it really doesn't do any harm. It's the venom that kills. And the venom that's injected by *this* snake is the most poisonous of all. The Bible calls it "sin." It kills, not only the flesh, but the soul and the spirit, as well.

One of the greatest dangers of this venom is the numbing effect it can have for some people. If you don't know you've been poisoned, you're not likely to take the Antidote. Some are aware that they've been bitten, but they've been so numb for so long, they just don't care. Others would be highly offended if one was to suggest they had been snakebit. Often, ironically, these are what we refer to as the "religious folks." They've been numbed to the point that it seems impossible to them that they could have been snakebit along the way. They just feel too darn good about themselves to have venom running through their veins!

Which leads to another danger of this particular poison. For some, it produces a kind of "high." They enjoy the venom and the experiences that it can bring. While this side-effect is different from the numbing sensation, it does itself, numb in a different way. Instead of numbing one to the snakebite though, it numbs one to caring that they've been bitten. They know they've been snakebit. They just don't care. They may even *like* it.

There is some good news on the snakebite front though. One thing, strange as it may sound, is that everyone that has ever lived has been snakebit (with one exception, which we'll get to shortly.) While it's not a good thing that everyone has been snakebit, it's a good thing in the sense that it lets you and I know we're not the only ones. We have a lot of company. The even better news is that, yes, as previously stated, there is an Antidote!

But before we look at the Antidote, I'd like to share a few more snake stories from the Bible with you. Some of them you probably didn't even know were there! I promise you though, that this book isn't about snakes…it's not even about the venom they inject into your body and soul…it's about the Antidote. It's just that before you can understand the Antidote, you have to understand that you've been bitten and the danger you're in.

The second recorded snakebite is in the very next chapter of the Bible. Genesis, chapter four. If you're not familiar with the story of Cain and Abel, they were brothers. They each offered a sacrifice to God. God was pleased with Abel's sacrifice, but not with Cain's. There are many speculations as to why God was pleased with Abel's and not Cain's, and any one of them could be right or wrong.

Personally, I believe it's because Cain offered God "some of the fruits of the soil" and Abel offered "some of the firstborn of his flock." Cain offered "some of the fruits" while Abel offered "the *first*born." God was getting Cain's leftovers, but getting the *first*born from Abel. Whatever the reason was, Cain didn't like it. He began to get angry. And while he didn't realize it, that ol' serpent was wrapping himself around Cain's feet and crawling up his leg.

"If you do what is right, will you not be accepted? But if you do not do what is right, sin is crouching at your door; it desires to have you, but you must master it." (Gen. 4:7).

Well, just like we humans today, Cain failed to master it. The serpent that was crawling up his leg latched on to his hindparts and sunk his teeth right on in. Cain took Abel out to the field with that snake bouncing in the wind like a monkey's tail, and when they got to the field, Cain killed his brother. He'd just been snakebit!

A couple of chapters later, there are so many snakes around clinging to so many folks that God decided to destroy the world with a flood. Only Noah and his family were spared. A few chapters after that you can read the story of Sodom and Gomorrah. People were running around with snakes hanging off of 'em all over the place! God destroyed the cities with burning sulfur from heaven.

I'm not going to even attempt to show you all of the snakebites in the Bible. Number one, it would be pointless. Number two, you already know about most of them, even if you've never read the Bible. (How's that, you ask? Because you have your own snakes. Everyone does. And some of your snakes, you know almost as well as they know you.) Number three, I'm not here to help you understand the snakes in the

Bible. I'm here to offer you the Antidote for your own snakes.

The neat thing about the Antidote is this: it doesn't matter what kind of snake you have chewing on you. It doesn't matter how many snakes you have chewing on you. It doesn't matter how much venom is already running through your veins or how long it's been running through your system. The Antidote can take care of it all.

There is something I'd like to point out though. Something very important from the examples I just gave you concerning the snakebites. These snakes can't be destroyed. The flood didn't kill them. It killed everything else on earth, aside from Noah and his family…and, of course, the animals on the boat. But it didn't kill the snakes. The burning sulfur that rained down on Sodom and Gomorrah didn't kill them. It destroyed everything else. But you can't kill the snakes. They are eternal.

The good news is, while you can't destroy the snakes, you *can* destroy the power they have over you. The power of the venom. *You* can bring *them* under *your* dominion. But only with the Antidote. The Antidote is where the power lies. The power to destroy the power of the snakes. The power to counteract their deadly venom. The power to bring those snakes under your control and render them ineffective against you. But, and this can't be stressed enough, you can't do it without the Antidote.

Before I share the Antidote with you, there is one more very important snake attack we need to look at. It's found in the book of Numbers. Pay close attention here, because it's a very important link to the Antidote that we all need.

The Israelites had been in captivity for four hundred years. Enslaved by their harsh Egyptian masters. Moses, at God's insistence and with His direction, had come along and led them to freedom. During the course of their journey to freedom, though, they ended up being "sentenced" to wandering around in the wilderness for forty years for their lack of faith in the same God that had set them free. It may be interesting to note that we humans haven't changed much as the centuries have passed.

In any case, they were wandering around in the wilderness, and according to the Bible, this is what happened:

"But the people grew impatient on the way; they spoke against God and against Moses, and said, "Why have you brought us up out of Egypt to die in the desert? There is no bread! There is no water! And we detest this miserable food!" Then the Lord sent venomous snakes among them; they bit the people and many Israelites died." (Num. 21:4-6).

There were snakes all over the place! Folks getting snakebit. People dying. Not just a couple here and there, but *many* died. The Bible doesn't specify what "kind" of snakes, exactly. But in another way it does. It says "venomous" snakes. The same kind that bit Adam. And Cain. The same kind that infested the cities of Sodom and Gomorrah. *Venomous* snakes. The same kind of snakes we face today. *Venomous.* And people were dying. Just like today.

I think one of the reasons the Bible doesn't tell us if they were rattlers, copperheads, bamboo vipers or whatever, is simply because it doesn't matter. My belief is that there were all kinds of different snakes represented…just like we face a great variety of snakes today. And the snakes we face today are just as deadly as the ones that invaded the Israelite camp.

We humans think that in order to treat the bite of a rattlesnake, you need rattlesnake serum. But the Antidote that I'm going to share with you can cure *any* snakebite. Doesn't matter what kind of snakes you have hanging on to you! That's why the Bible doesn't specify. Because it just doesn't matter what kind you have…the Antidote covers them all!

Let's see what happened to the snakebit Israelites.

"The people came to Moses and said, "We sinned when we spoke against the Lord and against you. Pray that the Lord will take the snakes away from us." So Moses prayed for the people. The Lord said to Moses, "Make a snake and put it up on a pole;

anyone who is bitten can look at it and live." So Moses made a bronze snake and put it up on a pole. Then when anyone was bitten by a snake and looked at the bronze snake, he lived." (Num. 21:7-9).

The people went to Moses. Moses went to God. God said make a bronze snake and stick it up on a pole. "Anyone who is bitten can look at the snake and live." Notice, if you will, that "*anyone* who is bitten can look at it and live." It didn't matter what *kind* of snakebite one suffered from. Or *how many* snakes may have been hanging off of the person's flesh. Or how poisonous those snakes may have been. What mattered is that that person looked at the bronze snake on the pole.

At the same time, it didn't matter if the victim was rich or poor, young or old, male or female. It didn't matter if the victim was well known and a leader of the people, or if the person was known only by God and was a servant to all. It didn't matter if they were good or bad, clean or unclean. *Anyone* that was bitten and looked at the bronze snake lived. *Anyone.*

How were the Israelites healed? By looking at the snake on the pole. There was nothing to drink. No injection to take. No pills to pop. All they had to do was to have enough faith to look at the bronze snake. If they were bitten and looked at the bronze snake they would live. If they were bitten and refused to look at the bronze snake they would die.

"The Lord said to Moses, "Make a snake and put it up on a pole; anyone who is bitten can look at it and live.""

Who said it? The Lord. If the Lord said it, then it will be as the Lord said. What did the Lord say? He said to make a snake, put it on a pole and that anyone that was bitten could look at it and live. What did the Lord *really* mean when He made that statement? What He *really* meant when He spoke these words to Moses is this: that anyone that was bitten could look at the snake and live! (And you thought it was a trick question!)

What healed the snakebites? Two things working together.

#1. God's Word. God said that when they looked at the snake they would be healed. That's what He meant. It was His Word to the people. He's never broken a promise yet.

#2. Faith. Not a lot. Just a little bit. Just enough faith to make one raise his or her eyes to the snake on the pole. If they could have that little bit of faith…just enough to make them look… they would live.

Now, I'm not a genius, but I would think that whether they *really* believed that bronze snake could heal them or not, there were probably an awful lot of Israelites looking at it. Just in case. And the ones that did, lived. Keep in mind, that it wasn't the *bronze snake* that healed them. It was the act of *looking* at the bronze snake. It was the *faith* to look.

If it had been the bronze snake itself that healed all those people, there would have been no need to look at it. The snake was there on the pole whether they looked at it or not. The bronze snake was on a pole in the presence of the people. It was *there!* It didn't move whether they looked at it or not. It was *there*. The snake didn't heal anyone. *Looking* at the snake is what healed.

Faith. Obedience. God said *look* and they would live. The snake could sit on that pole all day, but if they didn't look, they didn't live. It was the *faith* to *look*. If they had the *faith* to *look*, then God honored His Word. That's all they had to do. Just have the faith to look. It didn't even have to be a *lot* of faith. Just enough to look at the bronze snake.

Had it been you or me, there's a very real chance that we'd be thinking, "How can that piece of twisted metal heal my snakebite?" That's not much faith. But I'd be willing to bet that we'd both be peering at that sucker for all we were worth. Just in case. And because we would have displayed that tiny little amount of faith, we would have lived. Just like they did.

Read those few verses again. Notice how it all turned out?

"So Moses made a bronze snake and put it up on a pole. Then when anyone was bitten by a snake and looked at the bronze snake, he lived."

When *anyone* was bitten by a snake and *looked* at the bronze snake, he *lived!* Imagine that! It was just as God said it would be! Will wonders never cease!

6.

Snakes are sneaky varmints. They glide along the ground in the tall grass. They hang from trees just waiting for some poor unsuspecting soul to wander underneath. Anyone that's ever worked on a farm knows that it's not uncommon to find a snake hiding out in the top of the barn. In years gone by, it was always wise to check the hole in the outhouse before having a sit-down. In other words, they're sneaky. They're conniving.

The snake that bit Adam and Eve was "more crafty than any of the wild animals" that God had made. They are devious. The Bible says they are "shrewd" (Matt. 10:16) and "cunning" (2 Cor. 11:3). You have to be careful with snakes. Otherwise you may end up getting snakebit.

There are few people that go snake hunting. Most encounters with snakes are quite by accident. At least from the human perspective. There are actually times when snakes are the hunters and we are the prey. They lie in wait until their instincts tell them the time is right, and…chomp! Someone gets snakebit. If you surprise or corner one of the slippery critters, the chances increase that you'll feel their fangs.

Then there are those other snakes. The ones you can't see. Like the one that bit Cain or the ones that invaded Sodom and Gomorrah. The ones that are all over each one of us every day, nibbling away and injecting their poison. Most of us, most of the time, are totally unaware of the feeding frenzy.

Some common snakes are lust, greed, jealousy, anger, envy, worthlessness and laziness. The gossip snake is especially menacing because most people that have been bitten by it don't realize they've fallen prey to its bite. They'll sit there and talk about each other and how the other is such a gossip, without it even crossing their minds that they're suffering from the very same symptoms. While this group of snakes wreaks its own kind of havoc, there's another group of snakes that's just as destructive, but in a different way.

These are a few of the snakes that can be found in the second group. Cancer, heart disease, diabetes, high blood pressure and the list goes on. Sure, we blame things we can explain (to some degree) for these snakebites, but no matter what we blame the symptoms on, they still come from the venom injected by our invisible snakes. It's easier for us, as humans, to find reasons and causes, than it is to admit we've been snakebit and take a little of the Antidote.

For instance, strokes are often caused by high blood pressure, which can be caused by cholesterol building up in the blood vessels, which is usually due to our diet and exercise pattern. That is *our* explanation. The Biblical explanation is simply that you've been snakebit. Now, I know that you don't recall seeing such a passage, but there's a very good reason for that. There isn't one! But if you'll bear with me, I'll show you how the Bible is full of snakebites, but even more importantly, I'll show you the Antidote!

7.

Let's start with the "father of all snakes" (I couldn't resist!). Who or what is he? That's an easy one. Most all of us know the answer to that one.

"...that ancient serpent called the devil, or Satan, who leads the whole world astray." (Rev. 12:9).

What else do we know about him? Well, let's see…
He's a big mouth bully.

"Your enemy the devil prowls around like a roaring lion looking for someone to devour." (1 Pet. 5:8).

The obvious thing to point out first, is that he is our enemy. In spite of the smoke-screens he throws up, in spite of his appearance, in spite of the "treasures" he offers, he is our enemy. We are at war with him, and he is at war with us. In war, there are casualties and suffering. But the more knowledge you have, not only about your enemy and his tactics, but about the weapons in your own arsenal, the fewer the casualties, and the less the suffering…at least in your own army.

Secondly, he intimidates. That's one of his greatest and most effective weapons against us. Intimidation. What is a roaring lion? Nothing but a loud, noisy, obnoxious cat. What harm can a loud, noisy, obnoxious cat cause? Absolutely none at all. You can't be harmed by a sound! A *feasting* lion might be something to be concerned about, but a *roaring* lion is nothing but noise.

It's not the roar that gives us trouble. It's when we hunker down in fear at the sound, and offer the lion our jugular, instead of getting back in his face and backing him down that we face trouble. He has so many victims that roll over and allow him to feast, that he doesn't need to stand there against one that fights back. It's too much trouble. He relies on our fear and his ability to intimidate. And usually, it works. If we, on the other hand, were to stand our ground, we'd see just exactly what's behind that loud noisy cat. Nothing. *And I can prove it!* Watch this:

"Resist the devil, and he will flee from you." (James 4:7).

See? That roaring lion is nothing but noise. Get back in his face and he'll take off running. Why? Because he knows there's nothing he can do. But we're getting ahead of ourselves here. As you can see, another characteristic of our snake is that he'll run from you if you resist. He's a coward. It's interesting to note, that he won't just walk away from you...he'll *flee*. Look up the word "flee" in the dictionary. You'll see the difference in walking away and fleeing. He *flees*. But only *if you resist*. Otherwise, he'll be munching on you for breakfast, lunch and dinner. He and his brood of snakes.

Another characteristic is that he is a tempter. As we know, he even tempted Jesus (Matt. 4:1). If he's got the audacity to tempt Jesus, what makes you think he won't bother you? Especially when he knows that, in your own strength, you are much weaker than the Son of God...much more susceptible to his wily ways.

It's interesting to note that in his spare time, he's a gardener.

"The field is the world, and the good seed stands for the sons of the kingdom. The weeds are the sons of the evil one, and the enemy who sows them is the devil..." (Matt. 13:38,39).

The field is the *world*. Not the earth, but the *world*. Our enemy sows seeds in the garden of the *world*. We live *on* earth, which is God's. But we live *in* the world, which is an entirely different thing. The *world* belongs to the enemy. The *world* is the battlefield between the Antidote and the snakes, with us in the middle. We're in the middle whether we choose sides or not. Whether we choose to fight or not. Whether we even realize there is a war on, or not...we are in the middle.

The world system belongs to the enemy. He sows his seeds in the field. Look around. Look at all the weeds around you. Weeds that give home to the snakes. The political system is a system of the world. The medical system, the financial system, the educational system, for example. Even the "religious" system that so many of us follow. They are all systems of the *world*. They are products of the world. If the world system belongs to God, then why do you think Paul said this?

"As for you, you were dead in your transgressions and sins, in which you used to live when you followed the ways of this world...." (Eph. 2:1,2).

"Do not conform any longer to the pattern of this world, but be transformed by the renewing of your mind." (Rom. 12:2).

If the *world* belongs to God, and if Paul was writing the Word of God, then he would be imploring us to *follow* the world system. Not steering us away from it. And if the world system doesn't belong to God, there's only one other person it could belong to...that old serpent, the devil. And what does he, the devil, do with it? Go back to Rev. 12:9.

He *"... leads the whole world astray."*

Paul is also telling us in Rom. 12:2 to *"be transformed by the renewing of your mind."* Why do we have such a hard time with our snakes? Because of our lack of knowledge...which is what this whole book is about: educating our brothers and sisters about the snakes, and, more importantly, about the Antidote.

What else do we know about that ol' serpent, besides the obvious? Did you know he was a father?

"You belong to your father, the devil..." (John 8:44).

This verse, in its entirety, reveals a lot, which we'll cover a little more in detail later. For now, it's enough to know that he is a father. His kids are all over the place. His snakes are all over the place.

We also know he's a schemer (Eph. 6:11). He sets traps for us (1 Tim. 3:7). He has power (Acts 10:38). We know he's a liar (John 8:44). He takes captives (2 Tim. 2:26). He's a murderer, a thief and a destroyer (John 10:10). He's an accuser (Zech. 3:1). He can enter people (Luke 22:3). He sifts people (Luke 22:31). He disguises himself (2 Cor. 11:14). He can work false miracles (2 Thes. 2:9). He has his own throne (Rev. 2:13) and his own "church" (Rev. 3:9).

He mimics God. To be repetitious for a moment, he's a father and a gardener...so is God. He has power, though it's limited, whereas God's is not. He can work false miracles, has his own throne and church. The antichrist, beast and false prophet in the book of Revelation are nothing but a copy of the Trinity. He knows the Bible. He knows the people in the Bible. He knows you and me.

That's enough about the serpent, for now. I don't want to give him any more credit than he already gets from most of us. I'd much rather move on to the Antidote! Before we check out the Antidote, though, it's important to take a closer look at the world and compare it to what God has to say. Maybe we can cut down some of those weeds that provide shelter to the snakes. You already know they're cowards. Exposing them goes a long ways toward keeping them away. That's why they like the weeds. It makes it easier for them to sneak up on you.

8.

"Do not love the world or anything in the world. If anyone loves the world, the love of the Father is not in him." (1 John 2:15).

See? Paul isn't the only one warning us about the dangers of the world. That ol' serpent the devil is just copying God again. God has given us the earth and the devil has given us the world. We get confused sometimes because the two exist at the same time and in the same place. It's hard for us to separate the two because of our lack of knowledge and understanding. Because the enemy's world exists, in part, on God's earth, we assume they are both one and the same.

"In the beginning God created the heavens and the earth." (Gen. 1:1).

God created the heavens and the earth. They belong to Him. They are His. Always have been (since their creation, anyway) and always will be. He has never relinquished control or given them away. They are His.

"Then God said, "Let us make man in our image, in our likeness, and let them rule over the fish of the sea and the birds of the air, over the livestock, over all the earth, and over all the creatures that move along the ground." (Gen. 1:26).

When God created Adam, He also gave His created man a gift. An exceedingly great gift. He gave Adam the world. The earth was already here. The world was born with Adam's creation. The responsibility of "raising" the world belonged to Adam.

"...and let them rule over the fish of the sea and the birds of the air, over the livestock, over all the earth, and over all the creatures that move along the ground."

Adam had dominion over the entire world. When Adam bit into the forbidden fruit, while that serpent was injecting his venom of sin, sickness, death and a host of other poisons, he was also sucking out Adam's God-given right of dominion over the world. That's what happens when you start trying to charm snakes. The tables can turn on you and you can end up being charmed instead. And while you're all glass-eyed, the serpent slips in and steals what's rightfully yours.

"For the foundations of the earth are the Lord's; upon them he has set the world." (1 Sam. 2:8).

"The earth is the Lord's, and everything in it, the world, and all who live in it..." (Ps. 24:1).

"Let all the earth fear the Lord; let all the people of the world revere him." (Ps. 33:8).

"Before the mountains were born or you brought forth the earth and the world, from everlasting to everlasting you are God." (Ps. 90:2).

"His lightning lights up the world; the earth sees and trembles." (Ps. 97:4).

"...before he made the earth or its fields or any of the dust of

the world." (Prov. 8:26).

"All you people of the world, you who live on the earth..." (Is. 18:23).

Are you starting to understand that the earth and the world are two different things? God created them both. While they are both His, at the same time, He gave *dominion* over the world to Adam as a gift. Adam gave it to the snake. Still not quite convinced? Think about this: did God love the earth so much He sent His only begotten Son? Nope. Read it for yourself.

"For God so loved the world that he gave his one and only Son, that whoever believes in him shall not perish but have eternal life. For God did not send his Son into the world to condemn the world, but to save the world through him." (John 3:16,17).

The earth doesn't need salvation. The world does.

"I am the light of the world." (John 8:12).

The earth already had a light. The greater to rule by day and the lesser to rule by night. All that's back in the beginning of the Bible. Go see for yourself. But the *world* ...that's different.

"The light shines in the darkness, but the darkness has not understood it." (John 1:5).

Where was the darkness? In the world. Isn't it neat that the earth is lit by the sun and the world is lit by the Son? Pretty cool, huh? Anyway, there's an awful lot in the Bible about the world. How about the prayer that Jesus made to God in John, 17:6-19). It's obvious that to Jesus the world was an enemy to those that belong to Him.

Why? Because the right to rule the world was handed over to

the snake in the Garden of Eden by Adam. It's now ruled by the "prince of this world" (John 16:11). And the prince of this world hates the Antidote and all who follow Him. Jesus wasn't praying for his disciples because they were "still on earth," but because they were "still in the world" (John 17:11). In fact, He never mentions the earth. He's not concerned with the earth. His concern lies with the world. The enemy's domain.

If you read on in John 17…the prayer for all believers…you may notice that the same is true of that prayer as well. Jesus isn't worried about the believers on earth, but about the believers in the world, which happens to be all of us, as the world is on earth. We confuse the two.

The earth is the planet. The world is the stuff on the planet. The earth provides the stuff that the world needs to survive. The earth was created by God, as was the world. But when He gave Adam dominion over the infant world, and Adam, in turn, gave it over to the devil, the world was raised in the ways of the enemy. It was twisted into something that it never would have been under God's rule. And it continues to be so today.

Let's take a little closer look at the world. See if we can't flush out a few snakes along the way. By the end of the book, you may just find that if there are any left lingering around, the Antidote is more than sufficient.

9.

From the time of Adam, up until the birth of Jesus, there was only one world. The world of the snake. But with the birth, life, death and resurrection of Jesus, God created a new world. A new world within the old one. He started over. And the new world would be the world that He had in mind when He created the first one.

Within the world of darkness there came a ray of light. And the snake didn't like it. That light was the birth of a second world. One over which the snake had no control. Dominion of this second world was given, even before He arrived on earth, to the Antidote (Prov. 8:23). The snake knew that if this second world survived he would lose a good chunk of his dominion, whereas if it failed, it would all belong to him forever. There could be no other new kingdoms after this one because Jesus was the last Adam (1 Cor. 15:45).

The first world was *created* by God. The second world was *born* of God. And, as we know, the second world not only survived, but flourished. What we don't understand is that now the world consists of two kingdoms. Before Jesus, there was only the one. Now there are two…and only two. The kingdom of God and the kingdom of darkness. Both co-exist on earth and they each have their own set of "laws." Our problem is that we not only have to choose between the two, but we have to learn to distinguish the two from one another.

Just like the world and the earth, both kingdoms co-exist in the same space at the same time. That's where part of our confusion lies. At the same time, the kingdom of darkness had a four thousand year head start on God's kingdom. Four thousand years to steep itself in tradition and to set itself in its own ways. Then along comes Jesus with this new kingdom that has its own way of doing things and everyone gets a little confused. Our problem is that we try to live a little in the old kingdom and a little in the new.

Let's look at it in the light of what we know so far. First of all, the devil is a gardener. According to what we've already read, we know he sows weeds. The world is his field. So before the birth of Jesus, this world was nothing but a field of weeds.

Secondly, the devil is a father. According to chapter one of Genesis, each thing God created reproduces according to its own kind. Corn breeds corn. Cows breed cows, etc. Therefore, it stands to reason that the ol' serpent bred...that's right. More snakes. (Just as a little side-note, he's still breeding. If you take a look around, you'll probably come to realize you know a few of them. A few of the more notorious latecomers might be guys like Saddam Hussein and Osama Bin Laden.)

I consider myself more country folk than city folk. Anyone that's spent any time in the country knows that when you come to a patch of weeds there are two things to take a little caution with when crossing that patch of weeds. Your grandmother would always tell you to be careful of snakes. Snakes like weeds. Weeds are great hiding places for snakes.

And after your first experience crossing a weed patch, you'd learn for yourself that all weed patches have briars and thorns hidden in 'em somewhere. Isn't it interesting that when Jesus was crucified, He was wearing a crown of thorns? Does that mean, by chance (or design) that maybe...just maybe He chose the thorns from the garden of weeds to become His chosen? And is it possible that, just as the mist (KJV) watered the ground in Gen. 2:6 to produce vegetation, that as Jesus hung on the cross, His blood "watered" the ground that produced the thorns? And as that ground was watered by the blood of the Lamb, could it be that the thorns grew into roses? Roses among the weeds. Both in the same field. Roses among the weeds and weeds among the roses. Two different worlds in one.

The Bible has several similar analogies, such as the one we looked at in Matt. 13:38, 39. Our problem as Christians is that we were raised among the weeds and we haven't learned the difference between their kingdom and ours. We're still trying to live a little in both.

Basically, what this means is, that we're always coming up against snakes. Some of them we can see and come to know quite well. Some of them may even be family members or friends. Others are invisible. Those are the dangerous ones. They can bite you and you may never even know it. Then you wonder why all the poison is running through your veins.

While the Antidote has saved you eternally, we often let that poison affect our lives here in this world. We don't have to be affected by the poison any more. That's what this whole book is about. Victory over the venom of the snakes. Learning to live less in the world and more in the kingdom of God. The less we live in the world…the more we live in the kingdom of God… the less the poison affects us.

Snakes don't like the light. Jesus is the light of the world. The closer to the Light we get, the fewer snakes we encounter. If we could understand how to live totally in the kingdom of God, we'd never have to worry about another snake. Never again, have to worry about the venom. We would still get snakebit because we live among the weeds. But, as we shall see, there's an Antidote that has destroyed the power of both the snakes, and their venom.

10.

The Antidote. Jesus. The Son of God. God manifested in the flesh. We, as Christians, generally accept the fact that He died for our sins. We accept the fact that He gave us victory over death, in that, when we die here in this life, we are "born" into eternal life. That our "death" is simply the beginning of a new life that will last forever.

What we fail to realize is that He did so much more than just those two things. What happened on the cross was that He provided everything we'll ever need…for the next life, yes, but also for this one. We claim to *believe* that. But we don't *live* it. Need proof? When is the last time your shadow healed someone (Acts 5:15,16)? How many people do you know that have been healed by someone's shadow? Precious few, I'd be willing to bet.

I'm not being judgmental. My shadow hasn't healed anyone either. I'm not just writing this book to help *you* learn. I'm also writing it to help *me* learn. Maybe between us, we can figure out how to live more in God's kingdom and less in the world. Maybe we can see our shadows healing people. Maybe we can see those who are starving to death, eat for three years from a handful of flour and a few drops of oil (1 Kings 17:12-1 Kings 18:1). Maybe we can see five thousand men and their families eating from five loaves of bread and two fish and still have baskets left over (Luke 9:14).

Maybe we can see our own "Lazarus, come forth!" (John 11:43, KJV). I know there are a lot of Christians that don't believe in modern day "miracles," and you're welcome to hold on to that belief, if you wish. But friend, if that's the way you think, you've been snakebit. There's a huge chunk of your flesh still living in the world. The Bible plainly says…

"Jesus Christ is the same yesterday and today and forever." (Heb. 13:8).

You're more than welcome to continue to live in the world I'm not trying to change your mind. It doesn't mean you're any less saved. But while you're lying out on the sidewalk waiting for someone else's shadow to heal you, I want to be one of the guys walking down the sidewalk sporting one of those shadows.

The question is, when that shadow passes over you, in your current frame of mind, will you even know that you've been healed? Or will you continue to lie there getting chewed on by snakes, wasting away and waiting for another shadow to pass? After all, you don't believe in modern day miracles. That spot on the sidewalk may be more comfortable for you.

But me, I'm tired of living in the world. I'm tired of being snakebit. I'm tired of seeing those I love getting snakebit. I'm tired of hearing about kids dying from this disease or that. I'm tired of hearing about people starving to death because they rely on governments to feed them instead of relying on God. I'm tired of seeing people that have so many snakes hanging off 'em that they're all bent over and hunched toward the ground from the weight. I'm tired of people being charmed by snakes into believing that there are no such things as modern day miracles.

I'm tired of people being drowned in debt because they're convinced there's no other way and no way out. I'm tired of people coming up on a roaring lion, toothless though he may be, and sticking their head in his mouth and down his throat, just because they don't know that he's nothing but noise. I'm tired of people walking around getting snakebit and thinking there's no Antidote. I'm tired of people being destroyed for lack of knowledge (Hosea 4:6). And I'm ready to stroll through the kingdom of God wearing a new pair snakeskin boots!

We all know there's only one way to get snakeskin boots, and that's to kick some snake butt! But the snake's butt has already been kicked! *We* think *we* have to be the snake hunters. What we need to understand is that Jesus has already killed the snake. All we have to do is skin the sucker and make us some boots!

Remember His final words from the cross?

"It is finished." (John 19:30).

What did He mean by that? He meant it was finished! What did He finish? Everything. He's already killed the snake! An interesting thing about snakes. If you chop off its head, it'll wiggle around for a good while before it actually ceases to move. Jesus has killed the snake. It's still got a while to wiggle, but the snake is dead. Jesus knows the snake is dead, and the snake knows it. The people that carry the doubts are us. That's why we're still living in the world instead of living in the new kingdom.

The kingdom of God.

11.

It's time for us to start chopping down a few weeds and flushing out a few snakes. Remember, the world is a field. A field of weeds. Dominion of it belongs to the serpent. It's a world of darkness...remember? The first chapter of John? The first thing we need in this world of darkness is light. And we know that Jesus is the light.

What else do we know about the world? Would you believe me if I told you the whole world is a lie? Now, I realize that's a bold statement, and to be quite honest, the revelation of that truth left me a little stunned when it was first revealed. What amazed me even more were some of the thoughts that followed that revelation. I can, however, back up that bold statement, not with *a* Scripture, but with an entire arsenal of Scriptures. We'll start by establishing the fact that the world does indeed, belong to Satan.

"But if our gospel be hid, it is hid to them that are lost: In whom the god of this world hath blinded the minds of them which believe not, lest the light of the glorious gospel of Christ, who is the image of God, should shine unto them." (2 Cor. 4:3,4 KJV).

"Now is the time for judgment on this world; now the prince of this world will be driven out." (John 12:31).

In the upper room at the Last Supper, as Jesus was speaking to His disciples, He made this comment to "dismiss" the group.

"I will not speak with you much longer, for the prince of this world is coming." (John 14:30).

"...because the prince of this world now stands condemned." (John 16:11).

"We know that we are children of God, and that the whole world is under the control of the evil one." (1 John 5:19).

"You, dear children, are from God and have overcome them, because the one who is in you is greater than the one who is in the world." (1 John 4:4).

The world is obviously not under God's dominion (although He retains ultimate control over it), because:

"Anyone who chooses to be a friend of the world becomes an enemy of God." (James 4:4).

"Do not love the world or anything in the world. If anyone loves the world, the love of the Father is not in him." (1 John 2:15).

"We have not received the spirit of the world but the Spirit who is from God, that we may understand what God has freely given us." (1 Cor. 2:12).

"For the wisdom of this world is foolishness in God's sight." (1 Cor. 3:19).

The world belongs to the devil. It is God's world, but He gave dominion over it to Adam, who in turn gave it to Satan. It is, at this time, the devil's world. Now, what do we know about the devil?

Remember John 8:44? A few words from that verse were used a few pages ago. This time, we'll look at the whole verse.

"You belong to your father, the devil, and you want to carry out your father's desire. He was a murderer from the beginning, not holding to the truth, for there is no truth in him. When he lies, he speaks his native language, for he is a liar and the father of lies."

Did you catch that? Did anything "click?" Read it one more time. See? I know you saw that part that says that he is a liar and the father of lies. After all, that part is pretty obvious. But did you see the part that says, *"...for there is no truth in him?"* There is *no* truth in him. If the devil says something, it has to be a lie, because *there is no truth in him*. None. *No* truth. Not even a little bit. It can't be stressed enough, that there is *no truth in him!* He *can't* tell the truth. If he were to *try* to tell the truth, he wouldn't be able to. Why? Because *there is no truth in him*.

The world belongs to him at the present time. It's his world. There's no truth in him. So what on earth makes us think there's truth in the world? The whole thing is a fake. It's a lie. It's a lie designed by our enemy to keep us from reaching our full potential in Jesus. Bear with me a bit longer, and I'll tie this thing up a little.

Before you start thinking I must be off my rocker, remind yourself what the purpose of the devil really is:

"...that ancient serpent called the devil, or Satan, who leads the whole world astray." (Rev. 12:9).

Remember? It's his purpose and intent to lead the whole world astray. Why do you think David wrote these words?

"Free me from the trap that is set for me, for you are my refuge." (Ps. 31:4).

Or these words?

"Keep me from the snares they have laid for me, from the traps set by evildoers." (Ps. 141:9).

Who is the greatest evildoer of all? Our enemy. That ol' serpent, the devil. A murderer from the beginning. The father of lies. The one who leads the whole world astray. The tempter, the deceiver, the schemer. So who do you suppose sets the most effective and the most deadly traps? And he uses his army of snakes to keep us so poisoned that we don't even realize we've been bitten.

"...As fish are caught in a cruel net, or birds are taken in a snare, so men are trapped by evil times that fall unexpectedly upon them." (Eccl. 9:12).

We've been trapped by evil times that have, most definitely fallen upon us unexpectedly, simply because of our lack of knowledge. How can one defend oneself against snakes if he doesn't realize the snakes are clinging to his body and soul? The times are evil, not just because the end is near, but because at the present time, the world is under the devil's dominion. And until Jesus comes again to take what's rightfully His, the times will remain evil...no matter how good and righteous they may appear.

Or how about this one?

"...that they will come to their senses and escape from the trap of the devil, who has taken them captive to do his will." (2 Tim. 2:26).

Wow! *"That they will come to their senses and escape"* from what? The trap. Whose trap? The devil's. Why did he trap them in the first place? He took them captive *to do his will.* I'm sure that none of us would willing do the devil's will. But that's what it says...he takes us captive to do his will. How about this?

""Be careful, or your hearts will be weighed down with dissipation, drunkenness and the anxieties of life, and that day will close on you unexpectedly like a trap. For it will come upon all those who live on the face of the whole earth." (Luke 21:34,35).

These are the words of Jesus, not mine. Though parts of this verse may not seem to apply to everyone, let's just take the part of that verse that does and look at that for a moment.

"Be careful, or your hearts will be weighed down with the anxieties of life, and that day will close on you unexpectedly like a trap. For it will come upon all those who live on the face of the whole earth."

And you thought it wasn't talking about you! We all live on the face of the earth! We all have anxieties of life! They're caused by the snakes. And if we're not careful, the venom can weigh us down and the day will close on us like a trap. How are we trapped?

Just like Adam and Eve. We get sucked into believing the lie. We're born into the world, and we stay there. Charmed by the snakes. Even once we're born into the kingdom of God, a big portion of our being remains in the world...charmed by the vipers. Taken by the lie. Trapped. Because we've been a part of the world so long, we've accepted the lies as truth and we're afraid to believe anything else. We've come to be comfortable in our world of darkness.

But just like it says in the first chapter of John, verses four and five:

"In him was life, and that life was the light of men. The light shines in the darkness, but the darkness has not understood it."

That's the thing, see? Our world of darkness now has Light. Now we can see the snakes. If we just know where to look. They're in the weeds. Where are the weeds? In the field of the world. Sown by the devil. We don't have to fear the darkness any more. And we don't have to remain in it. We *choose* to because it's more comfortable for us. We'd rather go around smelling the weeds and calling 'em flowers. Getting our noses snakebit. It's easier than stepping out in faith to romp around in the *real* flower garden.

But the Light is here. All we have to do is open our eyes. If you'll forgive me, we just have to shed a little "Light" on it. Are you ready to see how the whole world is a lie? How there's no truth in it? Are you ready to be set free from your trap, whatever it may be?

Then, read on…

12.

Let's recap some of the world systems. While these aren't all the systems of the world, they are some of the major ones. The financial system. The educational system. The religious system. The governmental system. The medical system. They're all systems of the world, designed by man to replace God. I know, I know. Another bold statement. But if you'll bear with me...

The financial system is one of the biggest and strongest of the traps, and one of the most convincing of the lies. It has affected us all, and continues to hold most of us captive. We're trapped. But we're trapped by choice. We've been sucked in by the world. Numbed by the venom of the snakes. Isn't it strange how Paul worded the second part of the following verse?

"It is for freedom that Christ has set us free. Stand firm, then, and do not let yourselves be burdened again by a yoke of slavery." (Gal. 5:1).

And here we are captive to the yoke of financial slavery. We forget that...

"...if the Son sets you free, you will be free indeed." (John 8:36).

The financial system is set up to lead you astray. It's purpose is to keep you in bondage. To keep you trapped. To limit what you can do in the kingdom of God by limiting what you can accomplish in the world. For instance...

It doesn't matter what position you hold, or what company you work for, your financial status is controlled by the financial system. You can't gain more wealth than the system is willing to give you. Even if you own your own company and have ten million dollars in sales a day, you are limited to that ten million dollars in sales a day. You are limited by the financial system to what the system will allow you to have. The system won't allow you to accumulate more wealth than you "earn." But what does God say?

"And my God will meet all your needs according to his glorious riches in Christ Jesus." (Phil. 4:19).

God will meet our needs according to *His* glorious riches. What riches does He possess? All of them. Everything is His. He doesn't have to depend on someone to buy His goods. He doesn't have to depend on an employer to supply Him with wages that are limited by a financial system. Everything is already His! And out of those riches, He will provide for us. But that's a hard faith to have. It's easier to be enslaved to a false world system that has charmed us with its lies. If we could learn to depend on God instead of the world, then we could also learn to follow this verse...

"Do not be anxious about anything, but in everything, by prayer and petition, with thanksgiving, present your requests to God. And the peace of God, which transcends all understanding, will guard your hearts and your minds in Christ Jesus." (Phil. 4:6,7).

That's the kind of freedom Jesus was talking about. But we allow the snakes to creep in and nibble on us a little and we're taken captive by the world. Yes, God gives us our jobs. He also gives us the ability to do those jobs. At the same time, we don't depend on *God* to provide. We depend on our *jobs* to provide. Because God gave them to us, and because He gave us the ability to do them, we think we're depending on Him to provide.

But we're still enslaved to the world system. It's the *job* that provides. At least in our minds. It's that subtle deception of the enemy. Just enough truth to make us believe it, without being truth. What happens when we lose our job? We run out to find another one before we "lose everything we have." We have bills to pay. We look for another job to provide for us. It's the financial system. The system of the world.

Ironically, it's the job we have that keeps us limited. If we make $20,000 a year, we're afraid to give that up to find something that pays $50,000. If we make $50,000 a year, it's good and stable. We're afraid to give that up to make $100,000 a year. We don't do better because we're afraid to give up what we have.

At the same time, if my job pays $50,000 a year, that's what I'm limited to. Sure, I may get a raise. I may get a hefty raise. I may get a raise of $10,000 a year. But I'm still limited in what I'm making. My employer, or the financial system, is still deciding for me. My wealth is not determined by God, or even by me. It's determined by what the system is allowing me to accumulate.

It's the financial system that charges me for my electricity and water. It's the system that I pay my mortgage or my rent to. It's the system that makes me pay for my food and for the food my family eats. The amount I pay for these things is determined by the false financial system of the world, which is, of course, a lie because there is no truth in it. But I keep paying into it, just like you do. It keeps me trapped.

The bank, the water company, the electric company, the oil company and the retail guys all think they have control over what our economy does. They're wrong. They're simply puppets of a fake world system that no one realizes is fake. It looks too good and too real to be fake. And rightfully so.

"And no wonder, for Satan himself masquerades as an angel of light." (2 Cor. 11:14).

Sure it looks like a good thing. In fact, it looks like a *great* thing! Because it's masquerading as an angel of light. But that doesn't make it any less false, or any less a lie. The truth is…or would be if we let it…that God provides all our needs *according to His glorious riches*. That's what the truth is. We're afraid He's not going to give us all we *want* or all we *think* we need. So instead of having all the riches of God at our disposal, we're content to settle for our simple little salaries and wages. It's sad.

Please don't misunderstand. The Bible clearly says that we are to work.

"For even when we were with you, we gave you this rule: "If a man will not work, he shall not eat." (2 Thes. 3:10).

"Make it your ambition to lead a quiet life, to mind your own business and to work with your hands, just as we told you…" (1 Thes. 4:11).

"Whatever you do, work at it with all your heart, as working for the Lord, not for men…" (Col. 3:23).

"He who has been stealing must steal no longer, but must work, doing something useful with his own hands, that he may have something to share with those in need." (Eph. 4:28).

"By the sweat of your brow you will eat your food until you return to the ground…" (Gen. 3:19).

Our problem is that we've been deceived by the world system into thinking we have to *earn a living*. What the Bible says is that we have to *work*. God has spent the whole Bible trying to explain to us that we can't *earn* anything from Him. He gives it freely. What can you do to earn salvation? Nothing. It's a gift from God. What can you do to earn healing? Nothing. It's a gift from God. What can you do to earn the power of the Holy Spirit? Nothing. It's a gift from God. So what makes us think we have to *earn a living?* The world. All God said was that we had to work to eat. He said nothing about earning anything.

We are kids of the King! We lack nothing if we depend on Him. We are not paupers! We are not servants! We are kids of the King. All that He has, which is everything, is ours! It's just that we've been blinded by the venom of the snakes. It keeps us limited in what we can achieve for our Father.

Read chapter 28 of Deuteronomy, for instance. Who is it speaking to? The Israelites. God's own. Do we not become spiritual Israelites when we accept Jesus? Paul says we do. Read the first four chapters of the book of Romans. In Galatians, Paul wrote this:

"If you belong to Christ, then you are Abraham's seed, and heirs according to the promise." (Gal. 3:29).

If God made His promises to the Jews, and because of our faith in Christ we are Abraham's seed (who by the way, is the father of the Jewish nation), then we are Jews through Abraham and heirs of the promise of prosperity.

What does God have to say about prosperity for His kids?

"The Lord will grant you abundant prosperity—in the fruit of your womb, the young of your livestock and the crops of your ground..." (Deut. 28:11).

"Walk in all the way that the Lord your God has commanded you, so that you may live and prosper..." (Deut. 5:33).

"...and observe what the Lord your God requires: Walk in his ways, and keep his decrees and commands, his laws and requirements, as written in the Law of Moses, so that you may prosper in all you do and wherever you go..." (1 Kings 2:3).

These are promises made under the old covenant. How much more of a promise are they under the new one? God has never, ever even hinted toward the idea that His kids should be poor! Many are, but it's because of the world system that has taken us captive. What if we were to throw a little Light on the darkness of the world system? What if we were to work and *believe God* for our provision instead of killing ourselves by *earning a living* in the way of the world?

"...prosperity is the reward of the righteous." (Prov. 13:21).

Who are the righteous? Those who live by faith (Hab. 2:4, Rom. 1:17, Gal. 3:28, Heb. 10:38).

Think about it for a moment. What is wealth? It's not money. Money is nothing but paper. In the old days, people traded gold and silver. That was wealth. They traded food and goods. That was wealth. But money? Let's see you eat it. Let's see you wear it. Let's see you breath it in or see it keep you warm in the winter. If you were to chuck a dollar bill into your woodstove on a cold winter's night, how long do you think you would feel the heat? Would you even feel it at all? Hardly!

But wood...that's wealth. A cord of wood will keep you warm for awhile. Gold, silver, corn, beans. That's wealth. Oil and gas. That's wealth. All of it comes from the earth. Not the world, mind you. The earth. It doesn't come from the devil's lie, it comes from God's abundant earth. God's wealth doesn't need money. God's wealth is real. God's wealth is *real* wealth. Not the fake stuff the world provides.

Money. Where does that come from? It doesn't spring from the earth. It's not grown or mined. It's *manufactured* by the world. False wealth. Does any of this make any sense at all to anyone? It's a lie. It's fake. And every single one of us is a victim of its venomous bite. Every single one of us. But, thank God, I'm learning. Thank God, He's shining a little Light!

If it's true that Jesus set us free…if it's true that He came to provide life more abundantly (John 10:10 KJV)…then answer me this: What is so abundant and free about spending 60 to 80 hours a week earning limited wages so that you can (hopefully) provide for your family? What is so abundant and free about just barely getting by? What's so abundant and free about working so many hours a week that you barely see your family? What's so abundant and free about being so tired (when you do have a few hours) that all you *really* want to do is nothing? And still, what do you have to show for it? What's left when the financial system gets through with you?

Can you provide an acceptable answer? Neither can I. Which means either God lied or we have a twisted way of thinking…and God wasn't lying. The devil is. And we choose the lie. That's messed up. We choose the lie. The charade of the angel of light over the true Light. See? The financial system is all part of the charade. The devil has no wealth. He doesn't need any. All he needs to do is keep us snakebit.

Ok, that's fine. But those verses are all Old Testament. What does the New Testament say about prosperity? Glad you asked! Aside from the previously mentioned verse that reassures us that God provides our needs for us out of His glorious riches, we find that He will also provide things for our enjoyment. Which, of course, is far different from our needs.

"Command those who are rich in this present world not to be arrogant nor to put their hope in wealth, which is so uncertain, but to put their hope in God, who richly provides us with everything for our enjoyment." (1 Tim. 6:17).

Verses 18 and 19:

"Command them to do good, to be rich in good deeds, and to be generous and willing to share. In this way they will lay up treasure for themselves as a firm foundation for the coming age, so that they may take hold of the life that is truly life."

How can one be generous and willing to share if they have nothing to give? That verse is talking to those who are rich in *this present world*. Maybe it's only the rich in this present world that have a special calling to be generous and to share so that *they* will lay up treasure for *themselves* for the coming age...so that *they* may take hold of the life that is truly life. Maybe we common folks aren't included in all the promises of the future, after all. Or maybe, just maybe we common folks have been deceived by the lie.

"In a loud voice they sang: "Worthy is the Lamb, who was slain, to receive power and wealth and wisdom and strength and honor and glory and praise!" (Rev. 5:12).

Wow! Did you ever realize that Jesus was slain to receive *wealth*? We knew about Him receiving power, wisdom, strength, honor, glory and praise. But did you ever realize *wealth* was included? Aren't we co-heirs with Christ (Rom 8:17)? How about the statement that Jesus makes in Matt. 10:8 that goes something like this:

"Freely you have received, freely give."

Freely we have received. What that means is that we have freely received. We don't see it with our eyes, so we don't believe it. But we have freely received because it has been freely given...just as we are to give freely. If He expects us to give freely, don't you think it's because *He* already has?

"Which of you, if his son asks for bread, will give him a stone? Or if he asks for a fish, will give him a snake? If you,

then, though you are evil, know how to give good gifts to your children, how much more will your Father in heaven give good gifts to those who ask him!" (Matt. 7:9-11).

(Isn't it interesting that He used the word "snake?") The point is we need to learn to believe the Truth and see the lie for what it is. A lie. Please understand that the point of this chapter is not wealth for the sake of having wealth. The point of this chapter is to expose the lie of the world and shed a little Light on the subject. If the enemy can keep us in debt, and under control of the lie, he can control what we *think* we can or can't do for God's kingdom.

It's not about the wealth. It's about where your faith lies. Is it in the world, or is it in Jesus? You're rich beyond your wildest imagination. Whether you believe it or not, is another thing. But your believing or disbelieving doesn't change the fact that your wealth is there. It only determines whether you'll see any of it in this life. Your wealth won't get you into heaven…and you won't take any of it with you when you go. But it's there for you to use while you're here…if you'll just follow the Light.

13.

Let's take a look at the educational system. Another charade. Another serpent that has charmed the masses. I'm not trying to belittle anyone for seeking "higher education." It's not my intent to belittle anyone for any reason. My intent is to expose the lies we live in for what they are, and to help you understand the truth of God. And the educational system that we live in is another of the devil's deceptions.

Even in grade school, what are we taught? We are taught what the *educational system* decides we need to learn. A group of *people* decides what classes we need to take in order to be accepted by society. They are well-meaning people. But they are just as charmed as we are by the serpent. The *system* decides what we need to learn and how much of it.

The same applies to the institutions of higher learning. If you want a degree in medicine, you must study and successfully pass the regimen of courses that have been determined for you by the educational system. Whether you like it or not, whether you agree with their choices or not, if you want your degree, you will study what they wish for you to study.

When the system decides that you have learned enough, they will issue your degree…which is nothing more than a piece of paper that tells the world you have completed your education to the satisfaction of the system. Again, I'm not trying to put anyone down for seeking higher knowledge, I'm simply trying to put a few things in perspective under the Light.

On top of that, as all systems are, it's interwoven with the financial system. The world systems are so entangled with each other that it would be impossible to try to separate them. These days there's precious little that you are capable of doing, according to the world system, without a degree. We go into a huge amount of debt as a people to advance our learning. Even the "free" education we're "entitled" to as children costs plenty.

At the same time, we all know people who have never been to school, or people who have dropped out, or people that have never attended college that have more knowledge than many "experts" we know. But we all know that when it comes down to the expert dropout and the expert graduate, which one will be successful in the world system.

Now before anyone starts jumping to conclusions, I'm not against education. I'm against the educational system of the world. Because it's a sham. And it's a shame. It sucks us deeper into the lie of the financial system and gives us a false sense of knowledge and wisdom…or "arrogance" might be a better word. But what does the Bible say about education?

"…and I have filled him with the Spirit of God, with skill, ability and knowledge in all kinds of crafts…" (Ex. 31:3).

"…Also I have given skill to all the craftsmen…" (Ex. 31:6).

How did Solomon, the wisest man to have ever lived on this planet, gain his knowledge? He asked God for it.

"Give me wisdom and knowledge, that I may lead this people, for who is able to govern this great people of yours?" (2 Chron. 1:10).

God not only gave him great knowledge and wisdom, but also *"…wealth, riches and honor, such as no king who was before you ever had and none after you will have."* (vs. 12).

Could it really be that we can learn simply by asking God? Could it really be true that His Spirit can and will impart knowledge and wisdom simply by asking? Or was that just for Solomon? Is this kind of knowledge one that's limited by another human being's education? Or is it of a *true* higher education?

"Teach me knowledge and good judgment, for I believe in your commands." (Ps. 119:66).

"Such knowledge is too wonderful for me, too lofty for me to attain." (Ps. 139:6).

Apparently it wasn't just for Solomon. And apparently it was pretty "lofty" stuff. It may not have been English or Math. But it was *real* stuff. Stuff that you won't learn in any school of the world. Not even in the seminaries. Even they are of the world. They're a part of the world's educational system. There's not a seminary on earth that will be teaching on the lie of the world any time soon. Not a one. Not one that will chop down the weeds. Not one that will kill any snakes. In worldly terms: would you rather learn from a man that *read* the Book? Or the Man that *wrote* the Book?

"The fear of the Lord is the beginning of knowledge..." (Prov. 1:7).

"...and if you call out for insight and cry aloud for understanding, and if you look for it as for silver and search for it as for hidden treasure, then you will understand the fear of the Lord and find the knowledge of God. For the Lord gives wisdom, and from his mouth come knowledge and understanding." (Prov. 2:3-6).

"For wisdom will enter your heart, and knowledge will be pleasant to your soul." (Prov. 2:10).

The Bible has a lot to say about knowledge and wisdom and where it comes from. How about some New Testament stuff? I know there are those who believe the Old Testament is obsolete, so here's a bit from the side of the Bible with the red letters.

"...For in him you have been enriched in every way—in all your speaking and in all your knowledge..." (1 Cor. 1:5).

Paul obviously believed the Corinthians had been enriched in knowledge through Jesus.

"To one there is given through the Spirit the message of wisdom, to another the message of knowledge by means of the same Spirit..." (1 Cor. 12:8).

"My purpose is that they may be encouraged in heart and united in love, so that they may have the full riches of complete understanding, in order that they may know the mystery of God, namely, Christ, in whom are hidden all the treasures of wisdom and knowledge." (Col. 2:2,3).

"If any of you lacks wisdom, he should ask God, who gives generously to all without finding fault, and it will be given to him." (James 1:5).

There is no school in the world that can or will teach you how to attain citizenship in the kingdom of God. There is no school in the world that can or will teach you how to reach a point in your life where your shadow heals the sick (Acts 5:15). Or, that can or will teach you how you can feed thousands of people with a few tiny fish and a couple of loaves of bread...and still have baskets left (Matt. 14:19-21). Or, that can or will teach you that you can part a sea and walk across on dry ground (Ex. 14:21,22). There's no school in the world that can or will teach you that stuff. They may teach you *about* it, but they won't teach you how to *get there!* They can't.

And if they could, they still wouldn't. That would give you too much power, here in the devil's world. It's his job to keep you limited. To keep leading you astray. He doesn't want you to have power. Or knowledge…because with knowledge comes power. At least he doesn't want you to have *true* knowledge. But he wants *you* to *think* you're gaining knowledge by going through the system. The charade.

And it works.

14.

How is the religious system a lie? It's not so hard to figure once you realize that the religious system is spawned by the educational system. It used to be that when a person was called by God to preach the gospel, they would preach the gospel. Now, they go to seminary. *Then* they preach the gospel. Only then, instead of preaching about what God taught them, they're preaching about what they learned in seminary...which is, of course, taught by man.

Again, it's not my intent to belittle or demean anyone. It's just the way the system operates. The whole purpose of the entire world system is to limit us in what we can and will do for God. The less wealth we have, the less our knowledge and understanding about God, the less our faith grows, and the less health we have, then the less we can do for God in *this* life. That's what it's all about. Keeping us limited. It's all about control. The snake wants to control us with his lies to limit what we can do for God. And he does.

We go to church on Sunday, study a couple of verses of Scripture and we're good to go for another week. We're saved. We know we're going to heaven when we die and that's good enough for us. But what about all the things we're missing? What about walking down the street and our shadows healing people? What about trusting God to provide for us? What about the abundant life that Jesus promised? What about all that?

Sadly, a lot of us think we already have it. Many others believe that promise is for the life to come once we reach heaven. Still others don't believe it exists at all...that it died out with the last of the apostles, and once we reach heaven we won't *need* these things. Please understand I'm not talking here about money. I'm talking about the abundant life. That may include wealth, but it's not about money. It's about the *abundant* life. The Garden of Eden kind of life.

Matt. 6:33 tells us to seek first the *kingdom of God* and His righteousness. *Then* all these things will be added to us. But why are we going to seek it? We think we already have it! Or we believe it's for the next life. Or we don't believe it at all. For those who think we already have the abundant life, I repeat my question from earlier...when was the last time *your* shadow healed someone?

If you believe the abundant life is for the "next" life, then I ask you to think about this: In the next life, we're already going to have all that stuff. The instant we hit heaven's door, all that abundance is ours...just for being one of God's kids. It's the inheritance. How can it be "added" to us if it's already in our possession? So it must mean for *this* life. In the sweet hereafter, we don't need it to be "added." It will already be ours. We need it "added" *here*...in *this* life.

If you think our abundant life died out with the apostles... then what does that mean for our salvation? Why didn't that die out with the apostles too? How can we be sure it didn't? If God placed our abundant life in the past, or if it lies somewhere in the future...what good is it doing us now, when we need it? God never called Himself "I Was" or "I Will Be"...God called Himself *"I Am." "I Am."* Right now. Today. This moment. God *is*. The abundant life *"is."* We just have to seek it to find it.

But the religious system doesn't want us to know this. It wants to keep us thinking that it exists in the future. Or in the past. Or not at all. Or that we already have it. Because once we figure out it exists *now,* we may start seeking it. And if we start seeking it, we may find it. And if we can ever find it, think of the havoc we'll wreak in the devil's world. All that hard work he does goes right down the tube.

Most preachers won't preach it. Most congregations don't want to hear it. Everyone is complacent where he is. A good many of you who read this book are content to go to church on Sunday, let the devil and his snakes chew on you all week, and go back again next Sunday. Why doesn't anyone want to take a stick (shaped like a cross, incidentally) and beat that sucker over the head with it? Why are we content to let him get away with it? And a good many folks think that by going to church once or twice a week, they're actually *doing* something!

It's at the point that for a lot of people, if their preacher is preaching stuff they don't care to hear, that ol' boy won't be in the pulpit long. If he goes after 12:00 sharp, may the Lord help him, because he's gonna need a new job soon. Maybe a telemarketing job, where he can talk all he likes.

Church, for a lot of people, is not about God, it's about us. What *we* want to hear in *our* time frame. If God can't reveal it in thirty minutes on Sunday morning, we must not need it. We're saved. We're good to go. We go to church, we get ourselves seen by everyone, and we're good for the next six days. No wonder we have no power. No abundance. It sort of reminds me of the Pharisees and their behavior. We want the religion instead of the God. Be careful. Remember…it's not the religion that gets you into heaven.

"'These people honor me with their lips, but their hearts are far from me." (Matt. 15:8).

Please understand that it's not our preachers or our churches that are the problem. It's the religious system. Preachers and churches are as much victims as the people. Complacency is as much a part of the lie as the lie itself. If we're satisfied with where we are, we're not going to keep looking…or as Paul said in Phil. 3:12, we won't press on toward the kingdom. We'll just sit back and relax, satisfied that we're saved. We don't need the abundance. We don't want the power or the blessings. We don't care about eating meat...we're content to sip our milk from the bottle of the religious system until we leave this world (1 Cor. 3:1-4, Heb. 5:13, 1 Peter 2:2). We should be sick and tired of milk by now!

The religious system seems to be broken down into two factions. There are those that are saved and truly want a closer relationship with their Lord, and there are those who want to be seen as religious. The first group is in bondage by the system that tries to keep them on milk instead of feeding them meat. The second group doesn't need any kind of bondage. They aren't a threat to the world system anyway. In fact, it's safe to say they are allies of the world system.

Let's look at what Jesus had to say about the religious system of *His* day:

"Woe to you...you hypocrites! You shut the kingdom of heaven in men's faces. You yourselves do not enter, nor will you let those enter who are trying to." (Matt. 23:13).

"Woe to you...you hypocrites! You travel over land and sea to win a single convert, and when he becomes one, you make him twice as much a son of hell as you are." (Matt. 23:15).

"Woe to you, blind guides!" (Matt. 23:16).

"Woe to you...you hypocrites! You give a tenth of your spices—mint, dill and cummin. But you have neglected the more important matters of the law—justice, mercy and faithfulness. You should have practiced the latter, without neglecting the former." (Matt. 23:23).

"Woe to you... you hypocrites! You clean the outside of the cup and dish, but inside they are full of greed and self-indulgence." (Matt. 23:25).

"Woe to you...you hypocrites! You are like whitewashed tombs, which look beautiful on the outside but on the inside are full of dead men's bones and everything unclean." (Matt. 23:27).

(Just as a side-note, it's thought-provoking that Jesus referred to these same folks as a "brood of vipers" (Matt. 3:7, 12:34, 23:33) isn't it?)

Perhaps this is the most interesting verse of them all...

"Woe to you experts in the law, because you have taken away the key to knowledge. You yourselves have not entered, and you have hindered those who were entering." (Luke 11:52).

Did you catch that? Jesus was throwing some woe on the experts in the law. Why was that?

"...because you have taken away the key to knowledge."

Let that sink in for just a moment, will you? The fact that the religious system has taken away the key to your knowledge of God. If that doesn't bother you, the best advice I can give you is to throw this book away and keep doing nothing. You are right at home in your world. If it does bother you, there's hope.
That hope is Jesus.

15.

The governmental system. It's important to understand that this is not about any one governmental system, but about them all. Man was not designed to be ruled by a government, but to be ruled by God. The Israelites were the last to fall into this trap set up by the world system…the last to be snakebit in this area. Up to this point, they had been ruled by God through his prophets and judges.

"So all the elders of Israel gathered together and came to Samuel at Ramah. They said to him, "You are old, and your sons do not walk in your ways; now appoint a king to lead us, such as all the other nations have." (1 Sam. 8:4,5).

"But when they said, "Give us a king to lead us," this displeased Samuel; so he prayed to the Lord. And the Lord told him: "Listen to all that the people are saying to you; it is not you they have rejected, but they have rejected me as their king. As they have done from the day I brought them up out of Egypt until this day, forsaking me and serving other gods, so they are doing to you. Now listen to them; but warn them solemnly and let them know what the king who will reign over them will do."" (1 Sam. 8:6-9).

As you read the following verses, it's quite possible that you will see a lot of parallels with our own lives and our own governments today. But like the preachers and churches of the religious system, it's not the governments that are necessarily "bad," but the *system*. The governments, too, are victims of the world system. They are, after all, run by men. Men who are often ignorantly influenced by the snake. The snake that leads the world astray.

"He said, "This is what the king who will reign over you will do: He will take your sons and make them serve with his chariots and horses, and they will run in front of his chariots. Some he will assign to be commanders of thousands and commanders of fifties, and others to plow his ground and reap his harvest, and still others to make weapons of war and equipment for his chariots. He will take your daughters to be perfumers and cooks and bakers. He will take the best of your fields and vineyards and olive groves and give them to his attendants. He will take a tenth of your grain and of your vintage and give it to his officials and attendants. Your menservants and maidservants and the best of your cattle and donkeys he will take for his own use. He will take a tenth of your flocks, and you yourselves will become his slaves. When that day comes, you will cry out for relief from the king you have chosen, and the Lord will not answer you in that day."" (1 Sam. 8:11-18).

How many congressmen can you find in Washington that pay their bills from a $20,000 salary? Even with their six figure incomes and their high-level expense accounts, they determine every few years that they need a raise in order to survive, so they give themselves one. Where does that money come from? You and me. If you are someone who gets an annual raise at your job, compare their increase to the one you receive. Notice a difference? How different would *your* life be if you could give yourself a raise whenever you thought you needed one?

You and I provide far more than a tenth of our income to the government. Yet, we have no say in how it's used. If it's determined that our property would be better suited as a highway, even though we may have worked all our lives to wrench it from the hands of the financial system, we all know what happens to it. It becomes a highway. The property that we worked all our lives for.

Nor does it matter how much you paid for your house. You paid sales tax when you bought it. You pay property taxes every year. If you want to add on, you'll pay for a building permit, which is just another word for a tax that gives you permission to build *on your own property*. Even once it's paid off, skip a few of the property tax payments and see how long it remains yours.

Common sense dictates that the government needs money in order to function as a government. To provide roads, schools and other services for the people it was set up to serve. But if the government in 1 Sam. 8 was expected to operate off of a tenth of the increase of the people, shouldn't any government be able to operate off of a tenth? If God's kingdom is expected to operate off of a tenth, shouldn't this worldly kingdom be able to do the same? It could probably do so very easily, if not for the men that make it up.

If it's decided for us that our children are needed in the military, that's where they end up. Though we have "religious freedom," at least here in this country (for now), we can't pray in school or bring a Bible to class. A total stranger can pass by your house and be offended by a nativity scene and sue you in court...even though we have the freedom to express our beliefs...yet that same stranger can go home, turn on the television and see someone chopping another person into pieces and no one bats an eye.

Everything the government can control, it controls. And it *tries* to control the things it can't. There's that word again. Control. (The very word, "govern," means to control or rule over. "Government" is simply the body that carries it out.) Their purpose in the world system is to limit what you can do for the kingdom of God. And like the other world systems, it can't be separated from the pack. They're all tangled up too tightly with each other. They are simply separate parts of the same system...systems within the world system. They all have, in spite of some honest people that are really trying to make a difference, a pit full of corruption and greed breeding within them. *All* of them do. And the governments that are set up to serve the people always end up being served by the people...including the very people that make up that government.

It's important to understand that this is *not* an "anti-government" thing, though in another sense, it is. It's more an "anti-world system" thing. An anti-snake, anti-venom thing. It's about finding freedom in Christ and the kingdom of God...even within the world system.

16.

Finally, the medical system. This is one that's really got us wrapped around the ol' serpent's "finger." It feeds off the financial system, shoots venom into the educational and governmental systems and allows the religious system an excuse for its lack of power, faith and knowledge. A key weapon of the enemy.

Ironically, while the medical system is designed (from the human standpoint) to benefit mankind, just like the other world systems, it's a system that's full of death. They all *appear* to be beneficial. But they are all lies of the enemy and full of venom. This one though, the medical system, is especially so. Once again, I'm not against doctors or what they try to do for us in our state of weak faith. I'm against the *system*. It's just another strong deception of the enemy to keep us limited in our power. A "sick" Christian isn't usually as capable as a healthy Christian to perform for the kingdom of God.

The world system tells us of cancers, viruses, deficiencies and so forth. The Bible says:

"...and with his stripes we are healed." (Is. 53:5 KJV).

"This was to fulfill what was spoken through the prophet Isaiah: "He took up our infirmities and carried our diseases. "" (Matt. 8:17).

The devil would have us believe we get sick. The Bible says we've been healed and that Jesus *"took up our infirmities and carried our diseases."* Where did He carry them to? The cross. What happened to them? When He died, they died...right along with our sins. What we experience as Christians is not sickness, so much as it is a spiritual attack by the enemy, that manifests itself in a physical form. We, more often than not, end up believing the lie of the devil over the truth of God.

That ol' serpent has us so deceived that many Christians actually believe that sickness is sometimes God's will! That's a ridiculous lie straight from hell! Yes, it's true that God sometimes uses sickness to accomplish His will, but it's *not* because it's His will for someone to be sick. It's because...

"You intended to harm me, but God intended it for good to accomplish what is now being done..." (Gen. 50:20).

We look at Job and point to him to support our claims that God uses sickness. You don't have to point to anybody. We already know God uses sickness. He uses it all the time. But it's because we don't understand that sickness is a deception of the enemy. We accept the lie as the truth. That's why He uses sickness. Because we're sick!

Point to Job all you like. I'll point to Jesus. First of all, Jesus had not yet died for our sicknesses and infirmities when Job was afflicted. Secondly, go back and read Job again, my friend. God didn't make Job sick. He *allowed* the sickness, yes...He even *used* the sickness. But He didn't *cause* it. Who did?

"So Satan went out from the presence of the Lord and afflicted Job with painful sores from the soles of his feet to the top of his head." (Job 2:7).

Was it God's will for Job to be sick? No, it was God's will to allow Satan to test Job however he wished except for the taking of Job's life (Job 2:6). God uses sickness all the time, but that doesn't mean it's God's will for us to be sick. If it was His will for us to be sick, why did Jesus going around healing people? Why did Jesus send the disciples out to heal people (Luke 10:9)? Why did God allow Peter's shadow to heal *"all of them"* that were touched by it (Acts 5:15,16)? Why did Paul send out handkerchiefs that healed people (Acts 19:12)?

"...for I seek not to please myself but him who sent me." (John 5:30).

If Jesus was pleasing the Father by healing, then *how can it be God's will for us to be sick?* If it was God's will for us to be sick, why did Jesus heal us by His stripes? Why did He bear our sicknesses and infirmities on the cross? How can it be God's will to heal us *and* for us to be sick, both at the same time? That doesn't even make sense!

"...how God anointed Jesus of Nazareth with the Holy Spirit and power, and how he went around doing good and healing all who were under the power of the devil, because God was with him." (Acts 10:38).

Jesus *healed.* That's the first thing. Jesus *healed.* Who did Jesus heal? *"All who were under the power of the devil."* He healed *"all"* who were *"under the power of the devil."* Assuming that those Jesus healed were sick, then the sick were those who were *"under the power of the devil."* If it *wasn't* the sick that He healed, could He have *"healed"* them? So then, the sick are *"under the power of the devil."*

"The reason the Son of God appeared was to destroy the devil's work." (1 John 3:8).

Why would Jesus come to *"destroy the devil's work"* if it was God's will for us to be sick? He was doing God's will when He bore our sickness and infirmities on the cross ....when

69

He *"destroyed the devil's work"*...when He healed *"all who were under the power of the devil!" That* is God's will! It was God's will *then* for *those* people, and it's God's will *now* for *you!*

There are those that say God put doctors here for our benefit. To a degree, that's true. But it's because He knew we wouldn't have the faith to receive *His* healing. It's because He knew we would be deceived and led astray...believing the lie over the truth. That's why God uses doctors so often. Because of *our* lack of knowledge and faith in Him!

We're going to go back through a couple of these world systems and compare them a little closer to the Word of God. And we'll take a closer look at the Antidote for this massive pool of venom that has sucked us into the snake's realm and so deceived us and led us astray. But on leaving this chapter, I ask one thing...and it's a simple thing.

Next time you get "sick," say you're sick. Say you're under the devil's power. Say the devil's attacking you. Say whatever else you want to say...but please, please don't say it's God's will...not after the sacrifice Jesus made in order to destroy it.

You owe Him that much, and so do I.

17.

"Freely you have received, freely give." (Matt. 10:8).

Jesus wasn't just talking about money or wealth here. He was talking about wealth, healing, knowledge, the Holy Spirit... everything that God gives us, He gives freely. And we're to pass it on. The world has us so trapped and deceived that even we, as Christians, end up selfish and afraid.

Sure, we think we're generous. And we are, more so than the world. But how many of us would follow the command of Jesus to...

"Give to the one who asks you, and do not turn away from the one who wants to borrow from you." (Matt. 5:42)?

"And if you lend to those from whom you expect repayment, what credit is that to you? Even 'sinners' lend to 'sinners,' expecting to be repaid in full. But love your enemies, do good to them, and lend to them without expecting to get anything back. Then your reward will be great, and you will be sons of the Most High, because he is kind to the ungrateful and wicked." (Luke 6:34,35).

How many of us live by these words? Especially when most of us believe we're barely getting by and providing for our own families? And the reason? Because we're afraid if we give so freely, we (and our families) will lack. Because we don't trust God to provide for us out of the abundance of His glorious riches. Because we've been snakebit and led astray. The truth is, we've been deceived. We lack knowledge.

If a stranger knocked on your door and asked you for the last piece of bread in your home, would you give it to him? Knowing that the kids haven't eaten today, would you give that person that you've never seen before, and most likely will never see again, your last piece of bread? It's not likely. Because we're supposed to "provide for our families." But, the widow in 1 Kings 17 did exactly that. And look what happened! Her "last piece of bread" lasted for three years (1 Kings 18:1)!

"Be not forgetful to entertain strangers: for thereby some have entertained angels unawares." (Heb. 13:2 KJV).

Our problem as human beings is that we lack faith. We see with the natural eye, rather than the spiritual eye. If we "see" the "last" piece of bread on our counter, then we fall prey to the deception that we are giving away our last piece of bread. We don't consider the words of David…

"I was young and now I am old, yet I have never seen the righteous forsaken or their children begging bread." (Ps. 37:25).

We forget what God has promised:

"And my God will meet all your needs according to his glorious riches in Christ Jesus." (Phil. 4:19).

David has never seen the righteous forsaken or their children begging bread. Who are the righteous? Those who live by faith. Remember? Do you also remember that without faith, it's impossible to please God (Heb. 11:6)? Have you forgotten that

"We live by faith, not by sight." (2 Cor. 5:7)?

Do you recall that:

"Now faith is being sure of what we hope for and certain of what we do not see." (Heb. 11:1)?

If you have trouble living by these words, you're in good company. Elijah had that problem, too. He had just spent three years eating the "last" piece of bread with the widow and her son. He had just seen God destroy four hundred and fifty prophets of Baal and consume his own water-soaked offering with fire (1 Kings 18). And because one woman threatened to kill him, he took off running and hid in the dessert (1 Kings 19). In fact, verse three, says it like this:

"Elijah was afraid and ran for his life."

Peter had trouble living by those words, too. If you've forgotten, he not only denied Jesus three times, but there's the whole walking on water thing, too.

"Then Peter got down out of the boat, walked on the water and came toward Jesus. But when he saw the wind, he was afraid and, beginning to sink, cried out, "Lord, save me!"" (Matt. 14:30).

Did you see what it said? Peter was walking on water. But when he "*saw* the wind" he was afraid and started sinking. He saw the wind with his natural eye and was deceived, ever so briefly, by the lie of the world. He chose, for that moment, the false reality of the devil over the truth of Jesus. And what did Jesus do?

"Immediately Jesus reached out his hand and caught him. "You of little faith," he said, "why did you doubt?"" (vs. 31).

That must've hurt.

"You of little faith...why did you doubt?"

"You were doing great, Peter! Why did you start believing what you saw with your natural eye? Why did you choose the façade of the world over the reality of the kingdom of God? Why did you choose to believe the lie over the truth? How come you chose to live by *sight*, rather than by *faith*...even for just that brief moment in time? Why did you let that snake sink his fangs into you? Did you really think I would let you drown? *Why did you doubt?"* The world's "knowledge" teaches us that a human being can't possibly walk on water. The knowledge God teaches us is that *"nothing is impossible with God."* (Luke 1:37). So, why did Peter doubt?

The same reason we all do. It's hard for us to put aside our natural sight in favor of our spiritual sight. You "see" the last piece of bread. But Jesus fed thousands with a couple of "last" pieces of bread. You "see" the X-rays and the spots where there should be no spots. But Jesus said that by His stripes we've been healed. You "see" the sins that you commit every single day...the same ones you did yesterday, and the day before, and you realize what a worthless hunk of flesh you are. But God says:

"...by one sacrifice he has made perfect forever those who are being made holy." (Heb. 10:14).

Can you see how it works? The snakes are doing their best to bring you down and keep you down...to keep you pumped full of their venom of lies... *"to lead the world astray."* But God is trying to teach you the truth. That we don't have to live by the world systems. Yes, we have to live *in* the world...but we don't have to live by the lies. We can live by the truth that He provides...*if* we have the faith. We don't have to believe what we see with our natural eyes. We can believe with our spiritual eyes...if only we *will*.

If you want to provide for your family with abundance, you

have to live *by faith* and not by sight. While that statement includes material wealth, it is not limited to material wealth. Far from it! In fact, if it's simply material wealth you're seeking for yourself and your family, you need to double check your spiritual standing with God. Let's look at provision.

""Look at the birds of the air; they do not sow or reap or store away in barns, and yet your heavenly Father feeds them. Are you not much more valuable than they?"" (Matt. 6:26).

""And why do you worry about clothes? See how the lilies of the field grow. They do not labor or spin. Yet I tell you that not even Solomon in all his splendor was dressed like one of these."" (Matt. 6:28,29).

It's natural for us to "worry" about these things. But that's the whole point! We're not designed to live in the *natural* world, but in the *spiritual* world…the world of *faith*. What else does Jesus have to say on this?

""If that is how God clothes the grass of the field, which is here today and tomorrow is thrown into the fire, will he not much more clothe you, O you of little faith? So do not worry, saying, 'What shall we eat?' or 'What shall we drink?' or 'What shall we wear?' For the pagans run after all these things, and your heavenly Father knows that you need them. But seek first his kingdom and his righteousness, and all these things will be given to you as well."" (Matt. 6:30-33).

Wow! Think about that for a moment! First of all, if we allow ourselves to worry about such things, it's obvious that we have "little faith." Secondly, if we run around after all these things, *we're no different from the pagans*! Thirdly, God already knows we need them. And if we allow Him to provide for us, instead of chasing these things ourselves, He'll give us things of far more "splendor" than we can attain on our own.

But most importantly, all these things will be *given* to us if…and this is a big "if"…if we "*seek first his kingdom and his righteousness.*"

And finally, Jesus has this to say on the subject:

"*"Therefore do not worry about tomorrow, for tomorrow will worry about itself. Each day has enough trouble of its own."*" (Matt. 6:34).

Why not worry? Because God's in control. He's more than able, and more than willing to provide all our needs according to His glorious riches. Remember? But we have to *trust*. And we have to *seek*. We don't have to seek the provision. We have to seek God in order to receive the provision. Seek *first* His kingdom and His righteousness, and *then* all these things will be given unto you.

What is His righteousness? Can we ever be so righteous in His sight? Yep, we can. How? By having faith.

"*Abram believed the Lord, and he credited it to him as righteousness.*" (Gen. 15:6).

"…*"The righteous will live by faith."*" (Gal. 3:11).

That word just keeps popping up. Faith. How are people saved? By grace, through faith (Eph. 2:8,9). How are people healed? By faith (Acts 3:16). How do people please God? By faith (Heb. 11:6). In fact, it's impossible to please God *without* faith! How did David slay Goliath (1 Sam. 17:49,50)? Faith. How did the three Hebrew guys end up dancing in the fire that was meant to burn them to ashes (Dan. 3:22-25)? Faith. How did Daniel put the hungry lions (that were supposed to feast on him!) to sleep (Dan. 6:16-23)? Faith. How did Moses part the Red Sea and walk across on dry land (Ex. 14:21,22)? Faith. Faith, faith, faith. It's all over the Bible! Whenever anything at all happened, whenever there was a miracle, whenever God showed up, what brought it on? Faith!

"Show me your faith without deeds, and I will show you my faith by what I do." (James 2:18).

"As the body without the spirit is dead, so faith without deeds is dead." (James 2:26).

What does James mean? How can we show our faith by what we do? We can sleep peacefully while the rest of the world worries, because we know our God can and will provide. Having faith, without using it, is the same as having no faith at all. Faith. And every time we try to use it, there will be snakes there to nibble away at it…to try to poison it with their deadly venom. The neat thing is that…

"…the one who is in you is greater than the one who is in the world." (1 John 4:4).

It's so hard for us as humans to live by faith because of all the snakes. It's hard for us to understand that in order to receive abundance, we have to give freely. It doesn't make sense to us. But it doesn't make sense because it's the exact and total opposite of the *world*. Do you want abundance in your life? Think about it carefully, because it's a hard thing to accomplish. But if you *really* want it, I can tell you how to get it. It won't be easy. It requires that word…*faith*.

"Remember this: Whoever sows sparingly will also reap sparingly, and whoever sows generously will also reap generously. Each man should give what he has decided in his heart to give, not reluctantly or under compulsion, for God loves a cheerful giver." (2 Cor. 9:6,7).

I know. You probably weren't expecting that one. According to God's Word, in order to receive abundantly, you have to give abundantly. Just look what happens when you follow this instruction. This is verse 8:

"And God is able to make all grace abound to you, so that in all things at all times, having all that you need, you will abound in every good work."

Did you catch that? So that *in all things...at all times... having all you need...*you will abound in every good work. All because God is able to make all grace abound to *you*. But first, you have to trust Him enough to *give*. So what does your giving and abounding in good works have to do with you receiving abundance?

"Now he who supplies seed to the sower and bread for food will also supply and increase your store of seed and will enlarge the harvest of your righteousness." (Vs. 10).

Because He'll not only supply seed and bread, but will "*increase* your store of seed and will enlarge the harvest of your righteousness." That's what giving has to do with you receiving abundance. That's why it's so hard for us to do. That's why it requires faith. Give in order to receive? It doesn't make sense by the standards and systems of the world. Do you want to live by faith, or by sight? By faith, or by "what makes sense?" Because faith, as powerful as it is, seldom makes good sense.

Would you like to know what happens if you choose faith? If you choose faith over good sense...the way of the kingdom over the way of the world...then this is what you can expect:

"You will be made rich in every way so that you can be generous on every occasion, and through us your generosity will result in thanksgiving to God." (Vs. 11).

You will be made rich...*in every way*...so that you can be generous on every occasion. And that will result in thanksgiving to God. Wow! But there's more. Verse 13 says that if you have the faith to give so freely, it will cause men to praise God. Verse 14 says that it will cause men to pray for you…and that their hearts will go out to you…because of the *"surpassing grace God has given you."* Do you still want abundance? Do you *really* want abundance? It takes faith. Enough faith to give freely.

The world system bombards us with the notion that we have to look out for ourselves. Accumulate all you can and hold on to it for dear life. Save. Save for retirement. Save for the kids' college education. The more we save, the more we'll have to enjoy our later years with. The more we'll have to leave to our children once we leave this world.

The mastermind behind the world system has us convinced that this is the way to go. But it's nothing but poison. The deeper you become embedded in this world system attitude, the more wealth you are stealing from yourself…the more wealth you are stealing from your children. Again, this wealth includes material things, but it isn't limited to the material. This wealth includes things like faith, knowledge (*true* knowledge), wisdom and much more!

Do you want to leave a *true* inheritance of *true* wealth? Then you need to learn to live by faith. And faith comes by hearing. And hearing by the Word of God (Rom. 10:17 KJV). What is the "Word of God?" Actually, the Word of God is not a "what" but a "who" (John 1:1-18). Jesus. Get to know Jesus. Don't get to know *about* Jesus. But get to know *Jesus*. Exercise that faith of yours. Start small if you like, but start. And work it. Exercise it until it begins to grow strong. Stop drinking milk and start nibbling on meat.

Before long, you'll find an interesting thing beginning to happen. Before long, instead of the *devil* giving *you* hell all the time, *you'll* be giving it to *him*. Remember the account of the seven brothers in Acts 19:13-16? The brothers were trying to cast an evil spirit out of a man, and the spirit had this to say to them:

"...the evil spirit answered them, "Jesus I know, and I know about Paul, but who are you?""

If you'll recall, the seven brothers were beaten and ended up high-tailing it down the road...naked and bleeding.

"Jesus I know, and I know about Paul, but who are you?"

Do the evil spirits know *your* name? Or do they just chuckle a bit whenever you show up, and ask each other, *"Who are you?"* If the devil doesn't know you, I would challenge you to introduce yourself. But should you choose to do so, you should be prepared for a fight. And a fight means you might get a little bloodied up from time to time, and maybe even knocked down now and then...but you'll win in the end. You're in the fight anyway, whether you choose to be or not. You can keep being the devil's punching bag, or you can fight back. So go ahead. Introduce yourself. Give the devil a little hell.

After all, it *is* his anyway.

18.

The world seeks to keep you in bondage. The more rope you have wrapped around you, and the tighter it's pulled, the less you can wiggle around to smack away the snakes. We've talked a little about the financial system and how that ol' serpent can use it to keep you bound. Some of us will never get out of debt without intercession from God. I'm convinced that as long as we follow the world system, we will be under the control of the world's systems, the two most powerful being the financial and the medical systems.

We touched a little on how the world systems are so entangled with one another that it's pretty much impossible to separate one from another. The financial system is woven into every aspect of every system so tightly that it can't be pried away by human effort. And few other systems can draw you as deep into the financial system as the other powerhouse…the medical system.

The people that comprise the medical system are well-meaning people for the most part. It's not the *people* in *any* of the systems that make the systems our masters. It's the systems themselves. The people within the systems are simply people that are trying to make the systems work. But these systems will never work because they are systems devised by the enemy, and they are run by imperfect human beings. The medical system is no different.

For instance, doctors tell us that certain foods are bad for us. Fats can lead to high blood pressure, high cholesterol, and they're bad for the heart. The Bible says that Jesus bore our sicknesses on the cross. Why is it so hard for us to believe that? Why do so many people suffer from high blood pressure, high cholesterol and heart disease? Because to those people, these things are a reality. Those folks accept the lie as being the truth …and so it *becomes* their truth. In the case of the food we eat…I'll let the story tell itself.

"About noon the following day as they were on their journey and approaching the city, Peter went up on the roof to pray. He became hungry and wanted something to eat, and while the meal was being prepared, he fell into a trance. He saw heaven opened and something like a large sheet being let down to earth by its four corners. It contained all kinds of four-footed animals, as well as reptiles of the earth and birds of the air. Then a voice told him, "Get up, Peter. Kill and eat."
"Surely not, Lord!" Peter replied. "I have never eaten anything impure or unclean."
The voice spoke to him a second time, "Do not call anything impure that God has made clean."" (Acts 10:9-15).

"Eat anything sold in the meat market without raising questions of conscience, for, "The earth is the Lord's, and everything in it."" (1 Cor. 10:25,26).

"But food does not bring us near to God; we are no worse if we do not eat, and no better if we do." (1 Cor. 8:8).

"One man's faith allows him to eat everything, but another man, whose faith is weak, eats only vegetables." (Rom. 14:2).

The medical system, through the world's educational system has decided that certain foods are bad for us as humans. While the above verses are dealing more with the issue of "clean" and "unclean" foods, the same is also true of "healthy" and "unhealthy" foods. God created it all. Why should we think that He would create food for us to eat that would kill us? If you've lived on this planet long enough, you already know that what they say is "good" for us today will be "bad" for us tomorrow. Likewise, what they say is bad for us today will be good for us tomorrow. They change their minds every few years, depending on the current "popular" human theories.

The medical system, through the educational system, has also "learned" that "sickness" and "disease" are caused by "germs" and "viruses." That is the worldly explanation. The truth is, they are caused by the *serpent*. Remember? *"...all who are under the power of the devil?"* The truth is, if we know the *truth* we can come against him. If we fall for the lie, we're at his mercy...and mercy is not one of his better qualities. For example: Jesus and the disciples weren't worried about "sanitation."

"The Pharisees and some of the teachers of the law who had come from Jerusalem gathered around Jesus and saw some of his disciples eating food with hands that were "unclean," that is, unwashed. (The Pharisees and all the Jews do not eat unless they give their hands a ceremonial washing, holding to the tradition of the elders. When they come from the marketplace they do not eat unless they wash..." (Mark 7:1-4).

(Note that they washed because of ceremonial tradition. Their washing of hands had nothing to do with cleanliness or sanitation!)

"So the Pharisees and teachers of the law asked Jesus, "Why don't your disciples live according to the tradition of the elders instead of eating their food with 'unclean' hands?"" (Mark 7:5).

"Again Jesus called the crowd to him and said, "Listen to me, everyone, and understand this. Nothing outside a man can

make him 'unclean' by going into him. Rather, it is what comes out of a man that makes him 'unclean.'" (Mark 7:14,15).

Again, these verses speak of "uncleanness," but the same is true of "health." In fact, if you read the above verses again, and substitute the word "unclean" with the word "unhealthy," you may get a little better understanding. Our health is not dependant on what we eat, or on our sanitation practices. It is dependant on God and our faith, whether that faith is in the world system, or in God's Word.

Please understand, that this is not meant to be a statement against sanitation, but it's intended, instead, to point you from the "worldly" perspective toward the "kingdom of God" perspective. Sanitation is a worldly concept. Do you really believe that when Jesus fed the five thousand, that the whole group "gathered at the river" to wash their hands? It's stated twice in the preceding verses that hand washing was *"the tradition of the elders."* Man's idea, in other words.

"One Sabbath Jesus was going through the grainfields, and his disciples began to pick some heads of grain, rub them in their hands and eat the kernels." (Luke 6:1).

What are the odds of finding water in the middle of a grainfield? Again, this isn't intended to be against sanitation, but it's intended to help you understand that "sanitation" is just one of the worldly excuses for the devil causing sickness. It's the systems of the world that come up with all the "causes" of sickness in order to "lead the world astray."

When you're sick, it's important by the world system, to get the right medicine. The same is true of the kingdom of God. The thing we have to understand is that all sickness has the same root. Satan. There's only one thing that can get rid of Satan, and that's Jesus. If we can learn to get enough Jesus in our system, there won't be room for the devil or his sickness. That's where we fall short. Penicillin may treat the symptom, but the root is still embedded in your flesh, and in your spirit. What we have to realize is that we don't need the penicillin to treat the symptom…we need Jesus to cure the disease!

Many times, the medical system helps us in our journey. It's a good thing we have it, because we don't trust Jesus enough for the healing. But think about it. Some of the medications we receive from the medical system actually make us feel worse than the condition we're being treated for! Some of the medications are more harmful to us than the conditions they treat. That's why they put warnings of side effects on the bottle.

How about surgery? Can it really be that God intended for another human being to cut our bodies open and fiddle around with our insides? And then sew us back up like a pair of worn out jeans? But look how often we choose *that* path over the one God put in place…

"Is any one of you sick? He should call the elders of the church to pray over him and anoint him with oil in the name of the Lord. And the prayer offered in faith will make the sick person well; the Lord will raise him up. If he has sinned, he will be forgiven. Therefore confess your sins to each other and pray for each other so that you may be healed. The prayer of a righteous man is powerful and effective." (James 5:15-16).

"Worship the Lord your God, and his blessing will be on your food and water. I will take away sickness from among you, and none will miscarry or be barren in your land. I will give you a full life span." (Ex. 23:25,26).

When Jesus went to the pool of Bethesda and saw the invalid lying among *"a great number of disabled people,"* for some reason, He chose to heal that particular man (John 5:1-8). Why didn't He heal the rest? Only He knows. It could simply be that He just chose whom He chose. It's interesting that on this particular occasion, though, it was *Jesus* that approached the *invalid*. But whenever the *sick* approached *Jesus*, He healed them *all*. He's never turned anyone away that *approached Him*.

"News about him spread all over Syria, and people brought to him all who were ill with various diseases, those suffering severe pain, the demon-possessed, those having seizures, and the paralyzed, and he healed them." (Matt. 4:24).

Whenever someone approached Jesus, they were healed. It's that simple. It didn't matter if it was one person, like the woman that had been bleeding for twelve years (Matt. 9:20-22), or a whole crowd of people. Nobody walked away from Jesus still sick. Nobody. Jesus healed *"all the sick"* (Matt. 8:16).

"Many followed him, and he healed all their sick..." (Matt. 12:15).

"When Jesus landed and saw a large crowd, he had compassion on them and healed their sick." (Matt. 14:14).

"...and all who touched him were healed." (Matt. 14:36).

"Great crowds came to him...and he healed them." (Matt. 15:30).

"Large crowds followed him, and he healed them there." (Matt. 19:2).

"The blind and the lame came to him at the temple, and he healed them." (Matt. 21:14).

"...and Jesus healed many who had various diseases." (Mark 1:34).

"...and all who touched him were healed." (Mark 6:56).

" ...the people brought to Jesus all who had various kinds of

sickness, and laying his hands on each one, he healed them." (Luke 4:40).

"...and the people all tried to touch him, because power was coming from him and healing them all." (Luke 6:19).

"He welcomed them and spoke to them about the kingdom of God, and healed those who needed healing." (Luke 9:11).

And again, Acts 10:38...

"...and how he went around doing good and healing all who were under the power of the devil, because God was with him."

Those are just a few of the many passages that relate to the healing ministry of Jesus. They don't include the healings by Peter, Paul and the other disciples. Nowhere *in the entire Bible*, from page one all the way through to the last verse of Revelation, will you or anyone else find a passage of Scripture that says Jesus couldn't handle it...so He sent someone to the doctor. Nowhere in the Bible did *anyone* who came to Jesus to be healed, walk away still sick. Nowhere. Either you accept the Bible as your truth, or you accept the lie of the world as your truth. And if you accept the Bible, then you'll have to admit that...

"Jesus Christ is the same yesterday and today and forever." (Heb. 10:38).

If He healed *then*, He heals *now*. If He healed *them*, He'll heal *you*. If He healed *"all manner of sickness,"* then He *still does*. Our problem is that we've been taken captive by the serpent...poisoned by his venom...blinded by his lies. We've been led astray. Remember Rev. 12:9?

"...that ancient serpent called the devil, or Satan, who leads

the whole world astray."

Folks, we've been snakebit. And I'm tired of it. That's all. It's time for a little Antidote. It's time for a little truth. It's time for some Jesus to be slapped onto some fang holes so we can *be set free.* As long as the "world" keeps looking for "causes" and "cures," then the "world" is going to keep finding them. Because as long as it's looking for causes and cures, then it's not looking for the Antidote. And as long as it's not looking for the Antidote, then in the eyes of that ol' serpent, (who has dominion over the world), all is well. You can talk about germs and "defective" genes and whatever else you like. The cause of sickness is the devil and the cure is Jesus. It's that simple. That's what the Bible says.

And as long as that ol' serpent can keep us deceived, he will. If that means offering a tidbit of a "cure" now and then, he'll see to it that a "cure" is found. In terms of the "world," that is. That snake, that charmer…has only one goal in mind. To keep your eyes, and mine, off of Jesus. Because he knows if we ever get our eyes set on Jesus, the deception is over. And if we ever break out of that deception…then we can bust hell wide open! Just think of what we could do for the kingdom of God then!

"Worship the Lord your God, and his blessing will be on your food and water. I will take away sickness from among you, and none will miscarry or be barren in your land. I will give you a full life span."
(Ex. 23:25,26).

19.

Our whole problem, as humans, hinges on a couple of things. One is knowledge. Because of the world systems, we've been deceived and we lack knowledge. Which is the biggest reason this book was written. But with the knowledge, we also lack faith. Knowledge without faith is nothing but knowledge. If the knowledge is not applied, then what good has it done? And knowledge *can't* be applied without faith.

You can't apply knowledge to *any* situation without having the faith *to do something*…anything. You may *know* all you want to, that if you put your car key in the ignition and turn the switch, then your car will start. But if you don't have *the faith* to put the key in, or to turn it, then you, my friend, will be walking. So, if you have the *knowledge*…and if you have the *faith*…then you still have that one more thing to do. You have to *do something*. You have to *use* your knowledge and faith, or they're still no good to you or anyone else.

"In the same way, faith by itself, if it is not accompanied by action, is dead." (James 2:17).

"As the body without the spirit is dead, so faith without deeds is dead." (James 2:26).

You need knowledge. You need faith. And you need to use

them. If you put your faith in the world's systems you're destined to a life of bondage. At the same time, faith in God's kingdom brings freedom.

The world says save your money to accumulate wealth. God said, that in order to gain wealth, you have to give generously. The world entices you to borrow until you can't borrow any more…and by then, you usually can't pay it back, either! God said that He would provide our needs and provide for our enjoyment. And you don't have to borrow it…He *gives* it!

The world says you're sick. If you're not sick, there are so many things in the world, and of the world, that can make you sick, that it would be no surprise if you soon became so. God says that you've been healed. Not that you *will be*, but that you *have been*.

The world says the more knowledge you gain through its system, the more money you can make, the easier your life will be and the more prestige you will have in the eyes of your fellow man. God says there's only one true source of knowledge and He is that source. He also says that all of the world's knowledge will do you absolutely no good at all without His knowledge. In fact, He says that all of the world's knowledge, wealth and health will do you no good…without Him.

"What good will it be for a man if he gains the whole world, yet forfeits his soul?" (Matt. 16:26).

See, you don't just need God's knowledge. You need God. If you have God, you have everything you'll ever need. Knowledge. Health. Wealth. And the only way to get God is through Jesus.

"Jesus answered, "I am the way and the truth and the life. No one comes to the Father except through me." (John 14:6).

The snake wants to keep you in bondage to the world, and by doing so, he keeps you in bondage to himself. That's why most of us walk around carrying so many snakes on our backs. Snakes of doubt, self-worthlessness, fear, sickness, anger, debt; the list goes on. Those things don't come from God. If they don't come from God and His kingdom, that only leaves one person and one place they can come from…the serpent and his abyss.

Our problem is that we've been so deceived for so long, that it's very, very hard for us to live any other way. Most of us find it easier to walk down our familiar paths of deceit and destruction, but that's because it *is* easier! It's always hard to leave our comfort zone for what we feel is unknown territory.

We like to "see" where we're going, because it's so much easier to *see* where we're going, than it is to simply step out on the water in faith…like Peter did. We like to understand what's happening. We like to know what's going on. The thing that throws a monkey wrench into our philosophy is this: there's no faith involved in the familiar path. There's no faith in what we "see."

"So we fix our eyes not on what is seen, but on what is unseen. For what is seen is temporary, but what is unseen is eternal." (2 Cor. 4:18).

Just as there are two kingdoms in the world, the kingdom of light, and the kingdom of darkness, there are also two other realms that we live in at the same time. There's the visible realm, that we're all so familiar with, and the invisible realm. The seen and the unseen. Like the visible realm, the invisible is all around us. We just can't see it with our natural, or worldly eye. If you wish, you may deny its existence, but you're denying it doesn't change the fact that it's there. We're *used* to not seeing it… because, of course, if we could see it, then it wouldn't be invisible. That's where faith comes in.

A great example is the following event:

"Now the king of Aram was at war with Israel. After

conferring with his officers, he said, "I will set up my camp in such and such a place."

The man of God sent word to the king of Israel: "Beware of passing that place, because the Arameans are going down there." So the king of Israel checked on the place indicated by the man of God. Time and again Elisha warned the king, so that he was on his guard in such places.

This enraged the king of Aram. He summoned his officers and demanded of them, "Will you not tell me which of us is on the side of the king of Israel?"

"None of us, my lord the king," said one of his officers, "but Elisha, the prophet who is in Israel, tells the king of Israel the very words you speak in your bedroom."

"Go, find out where he is," the king ordered, "so I can send men and capture him." The report came back: "He is in Dothan." Then he sent horses and chariots and a strong force there. They went by night and surrounded the city.

When the servant of the man of God got up and went out early the next morning, an army with horses and chariots had surrounded the city. "Oh, my lord, what shall we do?" the servant asked.

"Don't be afraid," the prophet answered. "Those who are with us are more than those who are with them."

And Elisha prayed, "O Lord, open his eyes so he may see." Then the Lord opened the servant's eyes, and he looked and saw the hills full of horses and chariots of fire all around Elisha." (2 Kings 6:8-17).

Most of us have the same type of vision that Elisha's servant had. We can only see what's in the visible world. From time to time, we may hear or read a story where someone catches a glimpse of the invisible, but for the most part, we're stuck seeing with our natural eyes. What would happen if we could persuade God to allow the scales on our own eyes to fall off like the ones on Paul's eyes did (Acts 9:18) so that we, too, could see the real world?

Take, for instance, the widow and Elijah. The story can be found in 1 Kings 17. God told Elijah to go to the widow's house, which, of course, he did. The widow was getting ready to prepare her last bit of flour and oil so that she and her son could eat their final meal, then die, as that was all she had and there was a famine in the land.

As it turned out, when Elijah showed up at her house, something unexpected happened. She fed Elijah first, and strangely enough, still had enough flour and oil for herself and her son. But then the really weird thing happened. When she woke up the next morning, she found there was just enough flour and oil for another day. Every morning, for three years of drought, she woke up to find enough flour and oil for another day.

The point of this story, at this point in time, is not so much that God provided...though, indeed, He did. But, instead, to point out that what we see with our natural eye is often misleading. The widow saw her last bit of flour and oil. She and her son were preparing to die because that was the last of their food. But she was seeing with her natural eye.

Had she been seeing with her spiritual eye, she might have seen, instead, *"the hills full of horses and chariots of fire."* She might have seen her cupboards filled with enough flour and oil to last for the next three years. She just as well might *not* have. Maybe God created it fresh every day. But she *might* have. Just *maybe* it was there all along and she just couldn't see it.

Maybe the wealth God has promised us is lying right in front of us. Maybe the healing He has promised us is sitting in our lap. But we're too busy staring at an empty checkbook or looking at the doctor's charts to "see" His fulfilled promises right in front of our faces. We're so charmed and full of venom that most of us refuse to even consider it possible. Most of us accept the deception of the serpent without question. We assume that the promises of God were just for the "Bible guys."
If that's true, how then, are we saved? Or is that, somehow, the one exception that was also meant for us?

As a child, I can remember my mother telling me to eat everything on my plate. There were children starving in Africa. She would tell me too, how much God loves us. We'd go to church on Sunday and the preacher would tell us the same thing. God loves us. Then he would take up special "missions" funds to help feed the starving people overseas. There were always plenty of sick people to pray for, too. And for years, I wondered, "If God loves us all so much, why are so many people sick and starving?"

I suppose I must have been (and still am) one of those guilty of "blind" faith, because I had faith. I knew that whatever the reasons were behind all these suffering people that God loves us and that He has a reason for everything. But that question still bounced around in my mind. It was a question that I couldn't answer. For *years* I couldn't answer it. To be more precise, for two or three decades that question lingered.

If You love us so much, Lord, why are there so many people sick and starving? Why do I watch people I care about suffer and die? Why do others watch people that *they* love suffer and die? To be honest, there were times that I would get a little miffed at God, because I couldn't understand why someone would get sick and slowly die when He *promised* us that His healing *had already been given*. Or how people went without when He promised to provide all our needs. How could I trust Him to provide for *me*, when He obviously was not providing for others, even though He promises in His Word...in writing, and *in blood*, to provide for us?

I still can't answer those questions in my own wisdom. But God can. I know, because He answered them for me. And I'm more than happy to share the answers with you. Years passed. People died. People are still dying, by the way. They're still starving in Africa. We are still perishing for lack of knowledge. And I've come to realize that it hurts God to watch it, just as much...even more... than it hurts me. For even deeper reasons.

Anyway, one night, around midnight (I was a night owl in those days), I was sitting outside in the dark, just enjoying the quiet and the darkness. I wasn't thinking about anything in particular. In fact, I wasn't really thinking. Just sitting and enjoying the night...the dark and the quiet. I suppose there must be something to Psalm 46:10.

"Be still, and know that I am God; I will be exalted among the nations, I will be exalted in the earth."

As I sat there, "thinking" about nothing, God answered those questions for me, not because He had to, but because He chose to. Maybe He was tired of being blamed for something that wasn't His fault. Or maybe He just figured I had wondered enough, and He knew I would never figure it out on my own. Or maybe He answered them for me, so I could share the answer with you. I honestly don't know. But it was rather humbling. It illuminated my ignorance and my arrogance, and for a while, it left me speechless, misty-eyed and apologetic.

"They're starving in Africa because they depend on their governments to feed them, instead of on Me," He said in a quiet, gentle voice. "And those that suffer with sickness are depending on their doctors, instead of on Me."

And that's all He said. He didn't scold me, though He would have been quite justified in doing so. He didn't explain Himself any further. Not that He needed to. Not that I expected Him to. He didn't use words or a tone that implied that He might be angry or defensive. He was simply, out of His grace, answering the question that had been burning in my mind for so long, in a soft way...a way that my feeble little mind could understand.

While that's all He actually spoke to me, He brought to mind Elijah and the widow. He brought to mind the five thousand that were fed with five loaves and two small fish...and the four thousand with seven loaves and a few small fish. He brought to mind more than a few of the healings that were recorded throughout the New Testament. And He convinced me that our lack, whether food, health or anything else, is not His fault, but ours.

Once I got over my initial dose of humility, my anger turned from God to people. From the beginning of humanity, our Creator has been offering to provide all our needs. No *need* is too great. None is too small. No *person* is too great or too small. He's been holding these things out in the palm of His great hand, offering to each of us…waiting for us to reach out and take what He gives. For *centuries* He's been waiting.

He doesn't *sell* our provisions to us. He doesn't hold them over our heads or threaten to take them back if we don't behave a certain way. He simply holds His hand out and offers to *give* us whatever we need. And we turn to the world instead. Can you imagine how that must make Him feel? *What kind of creatures are we?* Yet, He offered even more. He offered Himself. And still, we turn away.

It didn't take long to realize that my general disgust and revulsion with humans was misplaced. Part of that disgust and revulsion was with myself, by the way. I, too, am a part of the human family, and I'm certainly no exception to any of this. Which is part of what disgusted me about humans. I didn't want to be like those people that didn't understand or have faith. I still don't want to be one. But I was. And I am. Not so much as I was, perhaps, but more than I care to be.

But I realized that, while part of it is our fault, the biggest problem is simply that we've been snakebit. We're victims of a common enemy. The serpent that roams the earth like a roaring lion. The loud noisy cat. The viper that fills our veins with his venom and lies. We're victims of a craftily created façade that we call the world. And, boy, have we been sucked in!

The neat thing about all this is something the enemy didn't realize at the time of the event. Even we, in this day and time, don't realize the magnitude of what happened. But one day, back in the days of Matthew, Mark, Luke and John, an awesome event unfolded. God, in His grace and mercy…God, in His great love for the undeserving human race…God, the Almighty Creator of all…the Alpha and Omega…provided an Antidote for the snake!

While that ol' serpent was curling around the feet of Jesus…while the blood of the Savior dripped from the spike driven through His feet onto the scaly head of the grinning snake…while the viper's forked tongue was flicking through the air, tasting its victim…smelling its victory, sinking its fangs into the bloody heels of the crucified God…as it slithered up the bloody, shredded, dirty, sweaty mutilated body of the Messiah, as He hung on the cross…while the "father of lies" was curling around the neck of the great "I Am," celebrating its greatest achievement of all…the spell was broken. The promise of Genesis 3:15 was manifested in the flesh. And the head of the serpent was crushed.

Light came pouring into the darkness. Truth destroyed the lie. *Real* truth became an option to the false "truth" of the world. The works of the devil had been destroyed. But like a snake here in the natural realm has a little wiggle left when you chop off its head, so the snake in the invisible realm has a little wiggle left. But only for a time. And I've learned that it's not God, and it's not people, it's the serpent that is the object of my wrath.

His deception has been so great and powerful for so long, that even today, many people live in his kingdom, rather than in the kingdom of God. Even Christians. Even myself. Because, in spite of the truth, in spite of the Light, we still don't understand. We haven't learned to shake off the snakes. We're so used to carrying them around, we don't know how to act without them. So we walk around with the Antidote pumping through our veins, and as fast as the Antidote is pumping in, we're pouring it out to make room for the venom. The Antidote is *there!* Now we have to learn to have the faith to use it to attack the poison of the viper. Not just in ourselves, but in each other…and then, in the world…the serpent's very playground.

But to do that, we need a little knowledge about the serpent and his tactics, which we've already briefly discussed. And we need even more knowledge about the Antidote. Last, but not least, we need the faith to act on our knowledge.

20.

Let's take a closer look at Jesus. My intent is, for the most part, to let Him speak for Himself. If He can't convince you that the power of the serpent has been broken, I can assure you, that I won't be able to do it either. *Please* listen to what He has to say. Listen closely. And if you listen closely enough, maybe you'll hear the serpent's head being crushed...or chains of bondage falling away. Maybe you'll hear the *real* truth.

First of all, it's important to know that Jesus did it all on the cross. There isn't part of it "left to be done." It has already *been* done. All of it. Everything.

"When he had received the drink, Jesus said, "It is finished." With that, he bowed his head and gave up his spirit." (John 19:30).

"This was to fulfill what was spoken through the prophet Isaiah: "He took up our infirmities and carried our diseases."" (Matt. 8:17).

"Surely he took up our infirmities and carried our sorrows, yet we considered him stricken by God, smitten by him, and afflicted." (Is. 53:4).

"He himself bore our sins in his body on the tree, so that we

might die to sins and live for righteousness; by his wounds you have been healed." (1 Peter 2:24).

"The Son is the radiance of God's glory and the exact representation of his being, sustaining all things by his powerful word. After he had provided purification for sins, he sat down at the right hand of the Majesty in heaven." (Heb. 1:3).

"For he bore the sin of many, and made intercession for the transgressors." (Is. 53:12).

"Therefore, there is now no condemnation for those who are in Christ Jesus, because through Christ Jesus the law of the Spirit of life set me free from the law of sin and death." (Rom. 8:1,2).

"Who is he that condemns? Christ Jesus, who died—more than that, who was raised to life—is at the right hand of God and is also interceding for us." (Rom. 8:34).

""Aeneas," Peter said to him, "Jesus Christ heals you..."" (Acts 9:34).

"...I want you to know that through Jesus the forgiveness of sins is proclaimed to you." (Acts 13:38).

"This righteousness from God comes through faith in Jesus Christ to all who believe. There is no difference, for all have sinned and fall short of the glory of God, and are justified freely by his grace through the redemption that came by Christ Jesus." (Rom. 3:22-24).

"Therefore, since we have been justified through faith, we have peace with God through our Lord Jesus Christ..." (Rom. 5:1).

"Not only is this so, but we also rejoice in God through our Lord Jesus Christ, through whom we have now received reconciliation." (Rom. 5:11).

"It is because of him that you are in Christ Jesus, who has become for us wisdom from God—that is, our righteousness, holiness and redemption." (1 Cor. 1:30).

"Examine yourselves to see whether you are in the faith; test yourselves. Do you not realize that Christ Jesus is in you—unless, of course, you fail the test?" (2 Cor. 13:5).

"But the Scripture declares that the whole world is a prisoner of sin, so that what was promised, being given through faith in Jesus Christ, might be given to those who believe." (Gal. 3:22).

"And the peace of God, which transcends all understanding, will guard your hearts and your minds in Christ Jesus." (Phil. 4:7).

"And my God will meet all your needs according to his glorious riches in Christ Jesus." (Phil. 4:19).

"For God did not appoint us to suffer wrath but to receive salvation through our Lord Jesus Christ." (1 Thes. 5:9).

"Here is a trustworthy saying that deserves full acceptance: Christ Jesus came into the world to save sinners—of whom I am the worst." (1 Tim. 1:15).

"For there is one God and one mediator between God and men, the man Christ Jesus..." (1 Tim. 2:5).

"Both the one who makes men holy and those who are made holy are of the same family. So Jesus is not ashamed to call

them brothers." (Heb. 2:11).

"And by that will, we have been made holy through the sacrifice of the body of Jesus Christ once for all." (Heb. 10:10).

"Grace and peace be yours in abundance through the knowledge of God and of Jesus our Lord." (2 Peter 1:2).

"If they have escaped the corruption of the world by knowing our Lord and Savior Jesus Christ and are again entangled in it and overcome, they are worse off at the end than they were at the beginning." (2 Peter 2:20).

"...and the blood of Jesus, his Son, purifies us from all sin." (1 John 1:7).

"...But if anybody does sin, we have one who speaks to the Father in our defense—Jesus Christ, the Righteous One." (1 John 2:1).

"Who is it that overcomes the world? Only he who believes that Jesus is the Son of God." (1 John 5:5).

"We know also that the Son of God has come and has given us understanding..." (1 John 5:20).

"For God so loved the world that he gave his one and only Son, that whoever believes in him shall not perish but have eternal life." (John 3:16).

""Worthy is the Lamb, who was slain, to receive power and wealth and wisdom and strength and honor and glory and praise!"" (Rev. 5:12).

"A man with leprosy came and knelt before him and said, "Lord, if you are willing, you can make me clean."

Jesus reached out his hand and touched the man. "I am willing," he said..." (Matt. 8:2,3).

"...The reason the Son of God appeared was to destroy the devil's work." (1 John 3:8).

"...He has sent me to bind up the brokenhearted, to proclaim freedom for the captives and release from darkness for the prisoners..." (Is. 61:1).

"So if the Son sets you free, you will be free indeed." (John 8:36).

"...and how he went around doing good and healing all who were under the power of the devil..." (Acts 10:38).

"Peace I leave with you; my peace I give you. I do not give to you as the world gives. Do not let your hearts be troubled and do not be afraid." (John 14:27).

"But as many as received him, to them gave he power to become the sons of God, even to them that believe on his name..." (John 1:12 KJV).

"I have given you authority to trample on snakes and scorpions and to overcome all the power of the enemy; nothing will harm you." (Luke 10:19).

"Jesus Christ is the same yesterday and today and forever." (Heb. 13:8).

What He did yesterday, He will do today and tomorrow. What He did for one, He will do for all. What He did for the leper, what He did for the adulterous woman, what He did for the demon-possessed man, what He did for Lazarus, Peter, Paul and John...

What He did for the five thousand, the four thousand, the centurion and his servant, what He did for Nicodemus, Zacchaeus, Mary Magdelene, the paralytic, the blind man, the deaf man and all the crowds that followed Him…

What He did for the synagogue ruler and his daughter, the woman at the well, the woman with the issue of blood…

What He's done for every person that's ever touched Him or been touched by Him…

He will also do for you.

21.

"'...I am sending you to them to open their eyes and turn them from darkness to light, and from the power of Satan to God, so that they may receive forgiveness of sins and a place among those who are sanctified by faith in me.'" (Acts 26:17,18).

The world is full of snakes. The snakes have a taste for human flesh, human souls and human spirits. Their venom is deception, lies and charms...lures of the world. Jesus is the only *real* truth. The only *true* Light. Please take the time to read the next verse carefully and to understand the truth behind it.

"...he has given us his very great and precious promises, so that through them you may participate in the divine nature and escape the corruption in the world caused by evil desires." (2 Peter 1:4).

The world is under the dominion of Satan at the moment. A gift to the devil from Adam when he ate the forbidden fruit. As we know, the ol' serpent is the prince of demons (Matt. 12:24). Since the world is under his dominion, it stands to reason that his brood of viper demons helps him rule. While it's true that a good many men have evil desires, I believe *"the corruption in the world caused by evil desires"* is speaking, not of man's evil desires, but the devil's evil desires *"to lead the world astray."* It's up to us to decide whether or not to fall into the corruption of the world, or whether to stand on the promises of God, through Jesus. To keep sucking down the venom, or to spit it out and drink in the Antidote.

With this thought in mind, it's interesting to note what Paul writes in 1 Cor. 10:21.

"You cannot drink the cup of the Lord and the cup of demons too; you cannot have a part in both the Lord's table and the table of demons."

Do you trust in the world systems, or do you trust in Jesus? Where does your wealth come from? Your healing? Your peace of mind? Your wisdom and knowledge? Most importantly, your salvation? Who provides for your needs?

"You cannot drink the cup of the Lord and the cup of demons too; you cannot have a part in both the Lord's table and the table of demons."

There are those who believe that God uses doctors to heal. There is not *one* passage of Scripture in the Bible that supports that theory. If your faith is in doctors to heal you, either *the doctors* will heal you, or they won't. Chances are, it won't be free. Chances are, you're going to suffer a little before your "healing" comes by their hands. Doctors are a product of the world. *Healing* is a promise from God. But you have to have the faith to turn to Him for that healing. Do you remember what Jesus told the two blind men that came to Him for healing?

"...According to your faith will it be done to you..." (Matt. 9:29).

Again, the question: is your faith in your doctor, or is your faith in your Savior? Which path will *you* choose?

"According to your faith will it be done to you."

Is your faith in your job? Or is it in your Jesus?
"According to your faith will it be done to you."

How about your wisdom and knowledge? Is your faith in the world system to "educate" you? Or is it in the Source of wisdom and knowledge?
"According to your faith will it be done to you."

How about your salvation?
"According to your faith will it be done to you."

Is your faith in your alarm system to protect you? In your air bag and seatbelt? Your police department maybe? And your fire department? Your military?
"According to your faith will it be done to you."

Who do you depend on for your daily needs? Yourself? Your government? Where does *your* faith lie?
"According to your faith will it be done to you."

Please understand that I'm not trying to be judgmental or condemning. I'm just trying to get your mind stimulated a little in your thinking. "World" vs "Jesus." The truth or the lie...the light or the darkness. Just giving you a little food for thought. I can only decide for me. You have to decide for yourself...*if* there are any decisions to be made. But again, only you can answer that question. For example:

"And a woman was there who had been subject to bleeding for twelve years. She had suffered a great deal under the care of many doctors and had spent all she had, yet instead of getting better she grew worse. When she heard about Jesus, she came up behind him in the crowd and touched his cloak, because she thought, "If I just touch his clothes, I will be healed."

Immediately her bleeding stopped and she felt in her body that she was freed from her suffering." (Mark 5:25).

Please don't misunderstand. I'm not trying to imply that we shouldn't go to the doctor when we're sick, or that doctors are "evil" or "demonic." What I'm saying, is that if our *knowledge* was accurate, and that if our *faith* was exercised, we wouldn't *need* doctors. God gave us doctors…but only because He knows we don't have the faith or the knowledge to receive *His* healing. Even we, who drink from the Lord's cup, sometimes steal a sip from the cup of demons…because our knowledge and faith are lacking. I don't want to steal any more sips from that filthy cup.

There are no Bible verses that teach us to work harder or longer if we want or need more wealth. None that teach us to spend more time in school to gain more "knowledge." None that teach us the "art" of yoga to gain peace of mind. What the Bible *does* teach, however, is that if we need anything…anything at all…all we have to do is ask God. And have faith.

He provides our needs. *He* gives us knowledge and wisdom. It's *through Him* that we get our peace of mind. Work and school, like doctors, are not "evil" things. But they are not *the source* for the things we seek. The things we seek (and the things we need) can only be provided by one Source. The tools of the world will keep us in bondage. But…

"…if the Son sets you free, you will be free indeed." (John 8:36).

The snakes of this world are all around us. They feed on us, day in and day out. And we let them. They latch on and don't let go. We walk around without even realizing they're there because we're so used to carrying them around. While we feel the weight because the heavy load is burying us alive, it doesn't seem out of place because it's always been there. We blame our fatigue on life. But what we're *really* tired from is carrying all those snakes!

I don't have all the answers. I wish I did. I'm not entirely sure how we can break away from the kingdom of darkness and into the kingdom of God. Except through faith. I'm not sure how we can break away from stealing sips from the cup of demons…or the world systems. Except by faith. I'm not sure how to step out of the visible realm and into the invisible. But I *do* know that just because we live *in* the world, we don't have to be *of* the world. Or live by the world's "rules." We can live, instead, by the promises of God…but only if we *choose* to.

And I also know this: the snake is dead. He may have a little wiggle left until his season is done…but he's dead. And whether we live like it in *this* world or not, I know that the Antidote has delivered us from the venom. And that we don't have to be afraid of the roar of the lion that seeks to devour us. Again, because of Jesus, the Antidote. Nor do we have to allow ourselves to be led astray, as the rest of the world is…because of Jesus.

And I know this, that if we can ever figure out this thing called faith, we have some special promises from the Antidote, Himself:

"I have given you authority to trample on snakes and scorpions and to overcome all the power of the enemy; nothing will harm you." (Luke 10:19).

If you'll allow me…we have authority to trample on snakes and scorpions and to overcome *all* the power of the enemy; *nothing* will harm us. While I believe this includes the little creatures we see slithering along the ground, I also believe that it was a promise made primarily concerning that ol' serpent, the devil and his brood. We have authority to trample on those snakes and to overcome *all* the power of the enemy…*if* we have the faith.

And…I know this:

"And these signs will accompany those who believe: In my

name they will drive out demons; they will speak in new tongues; they will pick up snakes with their hands; and when they drink deadly poison, it will not hurt them at all; they will place their hands on sick people, and they will get well." (Mark 16:17,18).

Again, while I believe this passage includes the snakes we see, I also believe that it includes those we don't see. When we drink deadly poison, it won't hurt us at all. Not the poisons of the natural world, nor the poisons of the invisible world. Not the deadliest venom the serpent can inject. Nothing the enemy or this world of darkness can manufacture. Not any kind of poison can hurt us. Unless we let it by our unbelief. We will place our hands on sick people, and…they will get well. Not *may* get well, but *will* get well. We'll drive out demons. Shake off a few snakes. Speak in new tongues. But again, these are signs that follow *"those who believe."*

All we have to do is believe. Jesus has already done the hard part. He did all that on the cross, so that we wouldn't have to. Yes, He died for our sins. But He died for so much more, too. What He did on the cross was *everything*. There's nothing left to do. It's already been done. He destroyed the works of the devil. Sin, sickness, poverty, death and anything else you may think of.

Maybe your snakes inject you with a poison that has you convinced you're worthless. God says you are worth the blood of Jesus. Maybe your snakes inject you with anger or jealousy. His blood is the Antidote. If your snakes inject you with lust, He died for that, too. If your snakes keep you in bondage to debt or sickness, those were included on the cross, as well. Fear? His blood covered all that. Insecurity? That, too, was dealt with. Greed? The cross. You name it, it was done. There on the cross.

"It is finished."

Remember? Jesus has already done the work. All we have to do is believe. We don't even need *a lot* of faith. Just enough to try a little of the Antidote. He's already provided all the rest. If you'll just let Him deal with your snakebites…

22.

There's a story I'd like to share with you again before we part ways. It's one that you read a few pages back. If you would be so kind as to forgive me for being repetitious...but it's important enough to remind you of just one more time. Remember that this story took place long before the cross...centuries before the cross, in fact. But at the time that this event took place, God already knew we would be facing our own snakes today ...which is why the story unfolded as it did. And this time, I'll share with you... "the rest of the story."

As you may recall, it's a story about snakes. And, as you may recall, while these aren't the same snakes that you and I deal with today, they are of a very similar nature. They were venomous. Deadly. Just like those that you and I face.

"But the people grew impatient on the way; they spoke against God and against Moses, and said, "Why have you brought us up out of Egypt to die in the desert? There is no bread! There is no water! And we detest this miserable food!"

Then the Lord sent venomous snakes among them; they bit the people and many Israelites died. The people came to Moses and said, "We sinned when we spoke against the Lord and against you. Pray that the Lord will take the snakes away from us." So Moses prayed for the people.

The Lord said to Moses, "Make a snake and put it up on a

pole; anyone who is bitten can look at it and live." So Moses made a bronze snake and put it up on a pole. Then when anyone was bitten by a snake and looked at the bronze snake, he lived." (Num. 21:4-9).

This is a powerful story. Read it again, if you will. See if you notice a few things. Like the snakes we face today...in fact, like the snakes mankind has faced since Adam ate the fruit...these snakes that were among the Israelites were venomous. People were dying from snakebites...just like today. Friends, neighbors, family members...they were dropping like flies.

The people got together and asked Moses to pray to the Lord to take the snakes away, and Moses prayed for them. Now, here's an interesting thing. When Moses asked the Lord to remove the snakes, the Bible doesn't say that the Lord removed the snakes from among the people. What it says, is this:

"The Lord said to Moses, "Make a snake and put it up on a pole; anyone who is bitten can look at it and live."

God didn't remove the snakes. He left it up to the people to kill their own snakes. Nor did He promise that no one else would be bitten. But what He *did* do was far greater. He provided healing and safety for them while they each fought their own battles with their own snakes!

"Then when anyone was bitten by a snake and looked at the bronze snake, he lived."

When *anyone* was bitten...when *anyone* looked...when anyone *looked* at the bronze snake, he *lived*. It didn't matter who you were. If you were an "anyone" and you were bitten, if you looked at the bronze snake, you lived. Didn't matter if you were rich or poor, dark or light-skinned, young or old, male or female...if you were bitten and you looked at the snake, you lived.

Another important thing to notice is this: that's all you had to do. Simply look at the snake. You didn't have to *do* anything. If you did *absolutely nothing* but *look* at the snake…you lived. All you had to do was to have enough faith in what God was telling you to do, to lift your eyes and look at the snake. You could assume it was a bunch of nonsense and hype and wallow around in your self-pity as you died, or you could take a chance and glance at the snake…just in case. If you looked at the snake, you lived, and if you didn't, you died. That's all it took. Just that little tiny bit of faith to prod you into looking at the snake. That's it. Nothing else.

Finally, the bronze snake had to be mounted on a pole and placed among the people, high enough so that everyone could see it. After all, the snakes were everywhere. Those folks didn't know when or where they might be when they were bitten. One might not have the time or physical ability to run to the snake for healing. It had to be lifted up for all to see. No matter where they were in the camp, they could glance up and see the bronze snake, and if they had been bitten, they would live. Anyone. Just by looking.

Which brings us to the neatest part of the whole story. Years turned into decades, and decades into centuries. A solitary Man stumbles and crawls up a dusty street. In the dust, there's a trail of blood. It's His. On His back, there's a heavy wooden cross that He's dragging up the hill. That, too, is His. At the top of the hill, He is placed on that cross and nailed down. And it is here, that the story that began so long ago, finally ends…not just for the Israelites…but for each and every one of us. Strange as it may seem, as the story that began so long ago ends, a new story begins. A story far different from the old one. A story without snakes…*if* we're willing to believe.

Most of us, at some point in our lives, have at least heard John 3:16. We may have paid it no mind, but we've at least heard it. Or seen it during football games…or in newspaper advertisements. And it's a great verse. But it seems we always overlook John 3:14 and John 3:15.

"Just as Moses lifted up the snake in the desert, so the Son of Man must be lifted up, that everyone who believes in him may have eternal life."

Just as Moses lifted up the snake in the desert...*just as Moses lifted up the snake in the desert*...so the Son of Man must be lifted up, that everyone...*everyone*...who *believes* in him may have eternal life. He had to be lifted up high enough for everyone in the camp to see, no matter where we are or what we're doing. Anyone...yes, *anyone*...who looks will live. And all it takes is enough faith to get you to raise your eyes to the cross...and to the Man that took your place on it.

Which brings us to verse 16. The verse that you probably already know by heart. The one that tells us *why* He did it.

"For God so loved the world that he gave his one and only Son, that whoever believes in him shall not perish but have eternal life."

The cross. In truth, the cross did nothing but hold the Savior up to die. The Savior is the one that did everything. The Antidote. The Messiah. The Lamb of God. Jesus. *He* took the beatings. *He* took the ridicule and humiliation. *He* took the torment and the torture of having His flesh ripped away from His body. The spikes driven through His flesh and pinning Him to the cross like we might tack a note on a bulletin board. *He's* the one that hung there, impaled...the sun beating down on His tattered body...struggling to suck in one more breath. *He's* the one that felt the Father turn away...

He's the one that the snakes were clinging to that day. All of them. From eternity past to eternity future. Every snake that ever was or will be was fastened onto His body at that moment in time. The snakes of the body. The snakes of the mind. The snakes of the spirit. The visible and the invisible. All of them. Even the "king" snake...that ol' serpent, the devil. They were *all* there. All piled up on that one Man. They were there for one reason. To kill the Son of God.

But what those vipers didn't realize was this: as Jesus was dying on the cross and descending to the grave (Eph. 4:9), the cross still on His torn back…He carried each and every one of those snakes with Him. And just as He had struggled up the hill a few hours earlier, now He was struggling down the path to hell and hades with all those vipers clinging to His flesh. At first, they may have even been a bit playful as they slithered around in the pile, searching for a chunk of His body to chew on. They may have giggled a bit, as they felt His muscles growing weaker by the moment…as they felt Him dying from their deadly poison. After all, for these reptiles, this was a merry time. They were killing God!

But as those serpents began to realize what was happening… that Jesus was, indeed, giving them a free ride into the eternal abyss… the giggling stopped and *they* began to struggle. Just a little at first. But with each tortured step He took, they got a little more desperate…a little more fearful. Until they began to actually fight to escape, to abandon ship…to leap off His bloody back to freedom…and as they tried to jump off and slither away into the "weeds," He caught each one and fastened it back onto His own flesh. He wasn't about to let even one get away. With each step Jesus took toward the darkness, those slimy snakes struggled that much harder to break free, because they knew that if the Son of God ever got them into the pit…they would be in the pit for good.

They began to strike at His flesh with a new ferocity, as He crawled toward the lake of burning sulfur. As the stench filled their reptilian nostrils, and terror began to course through their scaly bodies, fear turned into panic. Hisses and screams filled the darkness. The sounds of the serpents. Just as He bore the lashes of the whips of the Roman soldiers, Jesus was now bearing the effects of countless terrified fangs ripping at His body…serpents squirming, fighting in sheer desperation to break free. The harder they fought, the deeper they bit into His flesh, the more they writhed trying to escape His grasp…the tighter His grip became. Until...

Kneeling at the edge of the pit, the snakes screeching in rage...Jesus began to pull them from His tattered body...one...by...one...and hurl them into the unquenchable fire to be tormented day and night forever. And the "king" snake? He was the last to go. As that ol' serpent, the devil, hissed in the face of the Messiah, the Son of God suddenly took a deep breath, mustered all of His remaining strength, and stood up straight. He gave a deep sigh and with a violent shudder, He shook that bloody cross from His back and stared the serpent right in the eye. The one who masqueraded as an angel of light...and the true Light. Face to face.

The fear in Satan's eyes...the rage...as Jesus picked up His cross and brought it down...crushing the head of the serpent...just as His Father had spoken in the Garden of Eden. The 'carcass' went over the edge and into the pit. The bloody cross behind it. The Savior raised His eyes and hands to heaven and declared...

"It is finished."

Unlike the snakes here, in the natural world, the ones Jesus tossed into the pit are eternal creatures. Even though they've been cast into the lake of fire, they have the ability to slither out of their snakepit and "roam the earth" just as they did in Job's day, "looking for someone to devour." At least for now...until the season of wiggling is over. (Someday, of course, they will be sealed up in the lake of fire forever!) The thing is they no longer have power over us...unless we *give* them that power. It's a matter of faith. Are we intimidated by the deceptions? By the wiggling of their 'carcasses?' By the noise of the "roaring lion?" Or do we stand on the truth of God's Word?

Just like in the story of Moses, God hasn't promised to take away the snakes. He hasn't even promised to keep us from being bitten. He has done something far greater.

He has given us the Antidote. Jesus.

He's already dealt with the snakes. All we have to do is to have enough faith to walk among them without fear. Remember what He told us:

"I have given you authority to trample on snakes and scorpions and to overcome all the power of the enemy; nothing will harm you." (Luke 10:19).

Shake off a few snakes. Have a little faith. He's already done the hard part. Next time you feel the fangs sinking into your flesh, do what the Israelites did. Look at the snake on the pole. Just don't be surprised when you find it looks a lot like a Man on a cross.

Go ahead.
Take a peek.
Live a little, won't you?

Thanks for taking the time to read this book. Feel free to visit my website at www.imonlywood.com and browse around.

Other available titles by this author:

Grease Spots & Mustard Stains

Hail, Ye Knights of the King
(Available in October 2007)

Available at Lulu.com, Amazon and most other major bookstores.

www.ingramcontent.com/pod-product-compliance
Lightning Source LLC
Chambersburg PA
CBHW031647040426
42453CB00006B/235